How to Ruin the United States of America

Also by Ben Stein

HOW SUCCESSFUL PEOPLE WIN:
Using "Bunkhouse Logic" to Get What You Want in Life

HOW TO RUIN YOUR FINANCIAL LIFE

HOW TO RUIN YOUR LIFE (hardcover)
(also available as an audio book)

HOW TO RUIN YOUR LOVE LIFE

HOW TO RUIN YOUR LIFE tradepaper
(comprises the three titles above)

HOW YOU CAN SELL ANYONE ANYTHING
(co-written with Barron Thomas)
(available April 2009)

THE REAL STARS: In Today's America, Who Are the True Heroes?

26 STEPS TO SUCCEED IN HOLLYWOOD . . .
or Any Other Business
(co-written with Al Burton)

✫   ✫   ✫

Also by Ben Stein and Phil DeMuth

CAN AMERICA SURVIVE?: The Rage of the Left,
the Truth, and What to Do about It

YES, YOU CAN BE A SUCCESSFUL INCOME INVESTOR!:
Reaching for Yield in Today's Market

YES, YOU CAN GET A FINANCIAL LIFE!:
Your Lifetime Guide to Financial Planning

YES, YOU CAN STILL RETIRE COMFORTABLY!:
The Baby-Boom Retirement Crisis and How to Beat It

YES, YOU CAN SUPERCHARGE YOUR PORTFOLIO!:
Six Steps for Investing Success in the 21st Century

✷   ✷   ✷

All of the above are available at your local bookstore, or
may be ordered by visiting the distributors for New Beginnings Press:

Hay House USA: **www.hayhouse.com**®
Hay House Australia: **www.hayhouse.com.au**
Hay House UK: **www.hayhouse.co.uk**
Hay House South Africa: **www.hayhouse.co.za**
Hay House India: **www.hayhouse.co.in**

✷   ✷   ✷

How to Ruin the United States of America

Ben Stein AND Phil DeMuth

NBP

NEW BEGINNINGS PRESS
Carlsbad, California

Published by: New Beginnings Press, Carlsbad, California

Distributed in the United States by: Hay House, Inc.: www.hayhouse.com •
Distributed in Australia by: Hay House Australia Pty. Ltd.: www.hayhouse.com.
au • *Distributed in the United Kingdom by:* Hay House UK, Ltd.: www.hayhouse.
co.uk • *Distributed in the Republic of South Africa by:* Hay House SA (Pty), Ltd.:
www.hayhouse.co.za • *Distributed in Canada by:* Raincoast: www.raincoast.com
• *Distributed in India by:* Hay House Publishers India: www.hayhouse.co.in

Design: Tricia Breidenthal

Library of Congress Cataloging-in-Publication Data

Stein, Benjamin
  How to ruin the United States of America / Ben Stein and Phil DeMuth. -- 1st
ed.
    p. cm.
  ISBN 978-1-4019-1869-9 (hardcover)
  1. United States--Politics and government--2001- 2. United States--Foreign
relations--2001- 3. United States--Economic conditions--2001- 4. United
States--Civilization--1970- 5. Popular culture--United States. 6. Religion and
politics--United States. I. DeMuth, Phil, 1950- II. Title.
  E902.S735 2008
  973.93--dc22
                                    2008004617

ISBN: 978-1-4019-1869-9

11 10 09 08   4 3 2 1
1st edition, June 2008

Printed in the United States of America

Contents

Chapter
One

Exile God
from Public Life

☆ ☆

In the Garden of Eden, God created a paradise for Adam and Eve. Through their disobedience of God's commands, Adam and Eve exiled themselves from this world and were forced to bring forth children in sorrow, and eat bread earned by the sweat of their brows.

With the settlement of America and the founding of the United States, God had his angels lower the flaming sword guarding the garden gates and gave Eden back to humanity. Our country started under God's watchful eye, and its citizens have prospered miraculously, living in freedom and comfort, surpassing all other nations in history.

Then, in a startling role reversal of Genesis, they conspired to kick God out of their garden. The small minority of the population that's explicitly atheist used their henchmen in the courts to banish God from public life in the United States. The 92 percent of the population that believe in God were forced to stand by as the courts expelled Him from the kingdom. The very mention of the word *God* became so controversial that it has become far more acceptable to discuss one's sexual habits or drug addictions in public. Someone pretty much has to win the Super Bowl or a Country Music Association Award to get away with invoking God.

The sentinels of the ACLU and their liberal minions keep God at bay—and He seldom intrudes where He is not welcomed. Instead of being faithful to the covenant under which we were founded, our nation has dropped the gracious protective shield that God offered to us. This seems an excellent start toward ruining the United States. It's such a dramatic departure from history that it seems capable of doing the job all by itself. For a while, we can ride around on bald tires, sustained by the religious capital built up by earlier generations of Americans. And when that wears out, we'll be riding on nothing at all.

If we look at those countries that were explicitly founded on the dismissal of God and principles of atheism (dressed up as Marx's dialectical materialism)—the (former) Soviet Union, (former) Maoist China, (former) Tito's Yugoslavia, Castro's Cuba, and Kim's North Korea, as well as Vietnam and Laos—what we notice is that these test tubes have been hell on earth for their inhabitants during their Communist tenure. Instead of the foretold "withering away" of the state, what was far more common was the withering away of the population as it was systematically starved to death by its leaders. Yet incomprehensibly, this model of a worker's paradise seemed to be the ideal for liberal intellectuals in the West right up through the 1930s (and it continues to be revered in some places even today).

When Stalin's purges became better known, Communism fell somewhat out of favor, but it was quickly replaced as the new secular darling by socialism (Communism lite). Now the ideals are lived out in the dying countries of the Old World like Denmark and Sweden, which make no religious commitment but have a groaning smorgasbord of social benefits that make our country's unfunded Social Security and Medicare liabilities look like certificates of deposit gathering interest in the bank.

America: The Judeo-Christian Nation

Given the prevailing hostility to religion among our educational and media elites, it's difficult to think ourselves out of the secular paper bag we live in today, back to the outlook predominant in our country at the time it was settled by our ancestors. To say that this worldview was religious is a considerable understatement: There was, in fact, no other view. It's like saying that people breathed air.

Consider the relationship between God and man embedded in the mission statement Instructions for the Virginia Colony, dated 1606: "Lastly and chiefly the way to prosper and achieve good success is to make yourselves all of one mind for the good of your country and your own, and to serve and fear God the Giver of all Goodness, for every plantation which our Heavenly Father hath not planted shall be rooted out."

Up the coast a few years later, the Mayflower Compact (1620), was joined by 41 of the Pilgrims before their landing near Plymouth Rock to "combine ourselves together into a Civil Body Politic, for our better ordering and preservation . . . and by virtue hereof [to] enact, constitute, and frame such just and equal Laws,

Ordinances, Acts, Constitutions, and Officers . . . as shall be thought most meet and convenient for the general good of the colony."

A total of 195 words long, it specifically mentions God four times and states that their purpose is planting a colony for the "Glory of God" and for the "Advancement of the Christian Faith." All this from a document that is often cited in defense of a strict separation of church and state. It would be better cited as evidence of the separation of America from England, since there was nothing in the Pilgrims' charter allowing them to govern themselves.

The centrality of God to their purpose in America should not be surprising, since securing the freedom to worship God as they saw fit was the major motivator behind their journey. To them, the story of the Jews coming out of Egypt was not a casual Bible teaching. It was the central metaphor of their existence. They explicitly understood their voyage from England to be like the Jews' journey to Israel: a deliverance from oppression into a land of milk and honey.

While some early settlers were outcasts, prisoners, and derelicts (with slaves shortly to follow), most were glad to leave Europe behind. They were tired of the religious wars of the Reformation and Counter-Reformation, and had learned the hard way that a broad tolerance of sectarian differences was preferable to killing your neighbors over some putative doctrinal breech (a fundamental lesson that many followers of Islam have yet to discover). They'd had enough of European royalty, with its intrigue and decadence. They were extremely suspicious of popes and priests and emperors and kings who were always jockeying for power and using Jesus's church as a pawn in their acquisitive games.

If the Puritans and Pilgrims didn't want Euro-style civil and religious hierarchies, what did they want? They wanted to be left alone. Like Jan Hus and Martin Luther, they wanted a flat society where every person could have a direct relationship with God, unmediated by priestcraft. In their view, all people, whatever station they occupied in life, were equal in the eyes of the Lord, before whom they stood in the private hall of their own conscience, and whom they would answer to at the day of judgment.

They didn't worship Plato's Vision of the Good or Hegel's Absolute, but the Judeo-Christian God who sees into each human heart. As they were God's creation, their first duty was to their Father in heaven, and this claim was ontologically prior to all others—such as any competing claims from the state. This is why the early Christians trembled when asked to throw incense before a statue of the Roman emperor; this is why these European settlers, having crossed a dangerous ocean and having braved the loss of so many among them, found it necessary to circumscribe the power of the state over religious matters, and particularly a king of England who might have designs to establish Anglican rule over all of New England. Only a limited government could avoid becoming a secular God over its people.

As latecomers to the colonies fell away from the strong faith of the early Pilgrims and Puritans, great preachers arose to call them back into the fold. Jonathan Edwards's 1741 sermon "Sinners in the Hands of an Angry God" reminded them:

> The God that holds you over the pit of hell, much as one holds a spider, or some loathsome insect, over the fire, abhors you, and is dreadfully provoked; his wrath towards you burns like fire. . . . You have offended him . . . yet 'tis nothing but his hand that holds you from falling into the fire . . .

Michael Wigglesworth's poem "The Day of Doom" was the *Left Behind* of 1662, describing how people awaken one midnight to find the sun shining brightly and Christ unexpectedly returned to judge the quick and the dead. This stanza gives the flavor:

> *With dismal chains, and strongest reins,*
> *like Prisoners of Hell,*
> *They're held in place before Christ's face,*
> *till He their Doom shall tell.*
> *These void of tears, but fill'd with fears,*
> *and dreadful expectation*
> *Of endless pains, and scalding flames,*
> *stand waiting for Damnation.*

But if you don't get the message from that one, there are 223 more stanzas just like it. This was strong medicine—nothing like the weak tea that so many churches and synagogues serve up today.

The English Bill of Rights and the Toleration Act of 1689 eventually formalized the colonies' freedom of worship. Then John Locke's *Second Treatise of Civil Government* (dated 1690—70 years after the May- flower Compact established a social contract govern- ing by consent of the governed) advanced a theory of government based on a social contract by consent of the governed, as an alternative to the divine right of kings.

Locke asserted that people were endowed with natural rights of life, liberty, and property, and had the right to throw off governments that trespassed these rights. Marxist historians and their progeny, which include the standard secular historians of today, try to anchor the American Revolution in Locke. While this might apply to the French Revolution, it doesn't work for us. To be sure, the French conflict was founded on Locke, and especially the Rousseauian premise that man's inner nature was good and perfectible. These good French people then proceeded to guillotine an estimated 15,000 to 40,000 of their compatriots during the Reign of Terror.

By way of contrast, our founding fathers (following the Bible instead of Rousseau) assumed that people were sinners. Our *inalienable* rights to life, liberty, and the pursuit of happiness issued from God, not from Locke. Yet today, all one hears of is Locke and those few founding fathers whose faith was of a more attenuated, deistic kind (viewing God as a retired cosmic clock maker, with religion reduced to morality): Thomas

Jefferson, Benjamin Franklin, and Thomas Paine. Yet even these gentlemen were far more devout than many nominal Christians today. Paine, for instance, is said to have begged to be administered the Eucharist on his deathbed.

The signers of the Declaration of Independence and the Constitution overwhelmingly were practicing Christians. Certainly they were aware of the political ideas of their age; they were, after all, educated men. The Constitutional Convention was not the Council of Nicea. They were not metaphysicians or theologians (although a number of them were ministers, who were the thought leaders of their day). As Jacques Maritain said in *Man and the State,* "Far beyond the influences received either from Locke or the XVIIIth Century Enlightenment, the Constitution of this country is deeprooted in the age-old heritage of Christian thought and civilization." Maritain goes on to assert: "This Constitution can be described as an outstanding lay Christian document tinged with the philosophy of the day."

Interestingly, it's unlikely that there were *any* atheists in America at the time of the founding. As James Turner writes in *Without God, Without Creed: The Origins of Unbelief in America,* until the middle of the 19th century, ". . . failing to believe somehow in some sort of deity was not merely rare; it was a bizarre aberration." Karl Marx and Charles Darwin hadn't yet made atheism fashionable; it was a different world.

God's hand is evident in the intellectual superstructure upon which our country was built. In the Declaration of Independence, God is explicitly referenced as Lawgiver, Creator, and Judge, as well as Divine Providence. The equality of Americans is derived from the equality of all people before the Lord. Freedom to choose one's own leaders (democracy) is explicitly commended in the Hebrew Bible, and implicit in the free will that God gave to humanity.

At the same time, the Judeo-Christian tradition acknowledges that we're a sinful people whose impulses must be checked: In God we trust; all others pay cash. This leads to the necessity of a division of powers and checks and balances, rather than ruling from on high by godlike, divinely appointed philosopher kings or guardians and aristocrats who know best. It leads directly to a government of laws (as derived from the Bible) rather than a government of men.

It was widely believed that Providence had directly interceded in the creation of our country, in such singular interpositions (to use George Washington's phrase) as in our forefathers' safe passage across the Atlantic and in the course of events during the Revolutionary War. Mindfulness of this caused Franklin to reprimand the Constitutional Convention for not turning to prayer to ask God for guidance in their struggles. ". . . [H]ow has it happened, Sir, that we have not hitherto once thought of humbly applying to the Father of lights to illuminate our understandings? . . . Do we imagine that we no longer need His assistance?" he asked. Remember that Franklin is always invoked as the secular, worldly one among our founders.

So it shouldn't surprise us that the first Continental Congress opened with two hours of prayer on October 14, 1774, or to learn that the Supreme Court's first session began with a four-hour communion service. George Washington's Thanksgiving Proclamation, October 3, 1789, gives the flavor of the times:

> Whereas it is the duty of all nations to acknowledge the Providence of Almighty God—to obey his will—to be grateful for His benefits—and humbly to implore His protection and favor: And whereas both Houses have, by their joint committee, requested

me to recommend to the people of the United States a day of public thanksgiving and prayer, to be observed by acknowledging with grateful hearts the many and signal favors of Almighty God, especially by affording them an opportunity peaceably to establish a form of government for their safety and happiness:

Now therefore, I do recommend and assign Thursday, the 26th day of November next, to be devoted by the people of these States, to the service of that great and glorious Being, Who is the beneficent Author of all the good that was, that is, or will be . . .

The covenant of our nation with God required righteous behavior on our part. The notable failure was slavery. Had this been confronted directly at our nation's founding, there would have been no United States, since compromise on this issue at that time would have been impossible. It was left to the Civil War to right this wrong. Abraham Lincoln had campaigned for the Presidency on the platform that the God-given equality of man invalidated the Supreme Court's notorious *Dred Scott* decision endorsing slaveholding throughout the land. While the Civil War began as a battle for the Union against states' rights, it developed into a fight to free the slaves. Lincoln recognized this at the time of his second inaugural address:

Yet, if God wills that it continue until all the wealth piled by the bondsman's two hundred and fifty years of unrequited toil shall be sunk, and until every drop of blood drawn with the lash shall be paid by another drawn with the sword, as was said three thousand years ago, so still it must be said "the judgments of the Lord are true and righteous altogether."

Whatever God's role may have been, America has prospered and become a land of wealth, freedom, and opportunity.

Separation of Church and State

It should be clear that our nation's founders intended no particularly high wall between church and state. The phrase occurs no where in the Constitution. One day after passing the First Amendment ("Congress shall make no law respecting an establishment of religion, or prohibiting the free exercise thereof . . ."), Congress proclaimed a national day of prayer.

The people who passed the First Amendment weren't concerned about protecting citizens from exposure to anything pertaining to religion. There's no deep mystery, abstruse theology, or recondite political theory behind their intent. The words are so plain-spoken that almost anyone except a Supreme Court justice is capable of understanding them.

Our founders were concerned with protecting the church from the state—with gaining freedom for religion, not freedom from religion, as it were. More briefly, they did not want any one of the strains of Protestantism that were practiced here to be promoted to the level of a national church at the expense of the others. More briefly still, they did not want the Church of England. In the hands of kings and queens, this puppet church had used its secular and spiritual authority to squelch the Pilgrims and Puritans, forcing them to come to America to worship as they believed.

The Constitution's stricture was only against a national religion—states could still do as they pleased. At least six states had state-sponsored churches at the time the Bill of Rights was ratified, such as the Anglican Church of Virginia and the Congregational Church of Massachusetts.

The phrase "a wall of separation between Church and State" comes from a letter of Jefferson's explaining to some Baptists why he did not issue a Thanksgiving proclamation, as Washington and Adams had done before him. This is one phrase lifted from one of approximately 18,000 letters that the third President wrote. Jefferson's collected works span 30 volumes so far, and the editors aren't even up to his Presidency yet. If this were such a foundational idea to America, he possibly would have mentioned it more than once—maybe devoting, say, as much as one page to the subject out of the tens of thousands he wrote. Instead, he gave considerably more attention to the contents of his wine cellar and the topic of what sort of peas to plant in his vegetable garden. Had he known what a mess was going to be made from this one sentence, Jefferson would have ripped up his letter to the Baptists and issued a Thanksgiving proclamation instead.

Today, the "establishment" clause of the First Amendment ("Congress shall make no law respecting an establishment of religion") and the "free exercise" clause ("or prohibiting the free exercise thereof") have been pried apart by casuists, and the "establishment" clause is used as a club to beat the "free exercise" clause into submission. This completely violates the will of our country's founders, whose objective was simply to ensure that everyone could practice his religion free from government meddling.

Here are some of the milestones along the way:

- 1940, *Cantwell v. Connecticut:* The First Amendment is applied to states, and ultimately, to any state-funded institutions, like schools.

- 1947, *Everson v. Board of Education:* A former Klansman, Supreme Court Justice Hugo Black resurrects Jefferson's "wall of separation between Church and State" comment and promotes it to the judicial bumper sticker of the land.

- 1962, *Engel v. Vitale:* Prayer is outlawed in the classrooms.

- 1985, *Wallace v. Jaffree:* Nope, not even a period of silence.

- 1992, *Lee v. Weisman:* Clergy cannot deliver invocations, no matter how banal, at school functions. Establishes vital new constitutional right to "not feel uncomfortable."

- *Current:* Atheists are endeavoring to remove "In God We Trust" from our currency and "under God" from the Pledge of Allegiance. Perhaps a new pledge should replace that old, shopworn one? Here's a draft for your consideration: "I pledge of allegiance to myself to go placidly amid the haste, and may I never feel uncomfortable as I evolve under natural selection, as I do my thing, you do your thing, and the wisdom to tell the difference under Oprah."

All of this comes about because the Supreme Court, engineering a major power grab from the legislative and executive branches of our government, now feels perfectly free to ignore its mandate to interpret the Constitution as intended and instead freely fits the Constitution to present circumstances in whatever way makes the justices feel good at the moment. That this approach condemns the Court to trendiness and ties our laws into knots is but a small price to pay for the gratifying effect it has on the justices' egos. Cut adrift from all moorings, the Constitution now means anything they want.

Education in America was explicitly religious from day one. It wouldn't be going too far to say that at the time of our country's settlement, education was synonymous with Christian education. Within 16 years of the Pilgrim's landing, Harvard University was founded "To advance Learning and perpetuate it to Posterity; dreading to leave an illiterate Ministry to the Churches." The entire basis for compulsory public education was laid in the Massachusetts Bay Colony's 1647 "Ye Old Deluder Satan" Act. Because Satan's design was to keep people from having the ability to read the Scriptures, the act established schools throughout Massachusetts.

The importance of public education stemmed from the Reformation. Men had died to wrest the Latin Vulgate Bible away from the Catholic church and translate it into worshippers' native tongues. God had given men gifts of intellect and free will and conscience, and He left us the Bible. It was the duty of everyone to read and understand scripture according to their own lights and to forge their own relationship with God. Absent the ability to read the Bible, they were left at the mercy of whatever imposters might try to interpose between them and God. Thus, the Bible was the primary textbook in public schools. Even that old supposed secularist James Madison, author of the First Amendment, espoused the mandatory teaching of Protestantism in public schools at public expense because of the good habits and sound morals it would instill.

As a result of the antireligious bias of the Supreme Court, classrooms today have become petri dishes for social transformation, often making the evening news in the process. Any vestige of the Judeo-Christian tradition of worship is stomped on like a cockroach, while all other forms of religious expression are welcomed and the religion of secular humanism (that is, atheism) is the most welcome of all. Really, all atheistic creeds are worshipped: Marxism, existentialism, and scientific materialism. You are welcome to believe in just about anything so long as you don't believe in God. If a student dares to mention Jesus in her valedictory address, a U.S. marshal can be on hand to haul her off to jail (read David Limbaugh's book *Persecution* if you think we're kidding).

America is still a highly religious country. Statistics say that 92 percent of Americans believe in God, 85 percent identify themselves as Christian, 2 percent are Jews, and 1.5 percent are Muslims; while Hindus, Buddhists, and others are all less than 1 percent. Limbaugh's book collects a chilling description of the ways Christians get kicked around by the atheist minority, which is unable to tolerate the slightest mention of religion at school, at work, in the houses of government, or in the public square. Atheists are the outsiders, but now they use the law to marginalize Christians, while the media subjects Christians to endless ridicule and recrimination. Why? Because they can.

The liberals fantasize about a Christian theocracy with Pat Robertson as President, a government that will put cameras in our bedrooms and only allow coitus between married men and women practicing the missionary position, enforced by a strict (but secretly prurient) sex police. Isn't this what liberals are really worried about?

The great irony here is that all this public ridicule of religion has been made possible precisely by the latitudinarian attitude of the American religious (judge-not-lest-ye-be-judged) majority. While modern Christianity is a hothouse of tolerance, it's nevertheless viewed by outsiders as being stifling and repressive. In reality, this is nothing more than a projection of the liberal elite's own narrow and bigoted views on to their imagined enemy.

Now the spectacular trajectory of America through history, which shoots across the firmament like a bright meteorite, goes forward with the explicit connection of God and country severed. There's no more allegiance to God, to ethics, or to anything outside ourselves. This is a recipe for a return to the Hobbesian jungle—for more chaos, violence, and unbridled avarice. In other words, for exactly what we find today.

America, America, God shed His grace on thee.

Chapter
Two

Teach Americans
Contempt for America

☆ ☆

Having jettisoned the religious foundation of Western civilization like so much useless baggage, the next step toward securing the ruin of the United States should be to make sure that its institutions of higher learning teach its young people an attitude of contempt toward their nation and everything for which it stands. This will effectively hobble our country with an animus of feckless self-loathing to undermine everything it attempts.

By now this process is well under way and needs little in the way of further effort. First, Marxist historians gained ascendency, beginning in the 1920s, and recast our history from a story of American exceptional-ism to one of economic class struggle. In this new view, the Revolutionary War was reduced to a tax problem, despite the fact that taxation without representation didn't even make the "top ten" list in the Declaration of Independence (it charted at number 17 out of the 27 reasons presented).

The subjugation of the academy was an important step. As Marxist theoretician Antonio Gramsci under-stood by the 1920s, the Communist revolution had failed to ignite and spread across the Europe. For the West to fall, it would first be necessary to capture the institutions of its cultural hegemony.

By a stroke of good fortune, an educated class rose up to man the supply chains for this intellectual assault. From their redoubts in academe and the media, the ideas of atheism, exploitation, oppression, racism, sexism, homophobia, and fascism could be promoted until the culture lost its self-confidence and collapsed from within. While at first it might seem odd that peo-ple would want to destroy the same society that had brought them such education, prosperity, freedom, and leisure, this is exactly what happened.

In *Capitalism, Socialism and Democracy* (1942), economist Joseph Schumpeter foretold that under capitalism, the universities would educate a surplus of people beyond the numbers required to fill the available inputs in the labor force. These intellectuals would fall between the cracks: They would be too proud to perform manual labor, but also be unable to find professional employment commensurate with their tremendous sense of self-importance. This would leave them underemployed and disgruntled.

Trained foremost as critics, they'd constantly gnaw at the foundations of the society that created them because it sinned by overlooking their brilliance. As outsiders, their sharpest knives would be reserved for capitalism's symbolic representatives: businesses and businessmen. These envious intellectuals would attribute the businessman's greater wealth and prestige to factors such as exploitation, monopoly, fraud, and greed. Schumpeter termed these rationalizations "the autotherapy of the unsuccessful."

The recent statistics on higher education fully bear out Schumpeter's prediction.

Statistics

As a baseline, be aware that liberals and conservatives, Democrats and Republicans, are about evenly matched in the general population, in roughly a 1:1 ratio to each other. Here are some core samples on their representation in academe.

In 1995, *The American Enterprise* armed students at Cornell and Stanford University with a list of their faculty members and sent them to their local election bureaus to tally the party registrations of their professors. They ended up locating 199 from Cornell and 186 from Stanford, all representing a variety of departments. At Cornell, the ratio was 171 Democrats versus 7 Republicans (24:1). At Stanford, it was 163 Democrats versus 17 Republicans (10:1).

In 2001, the same magazine sought to replicate their findings at 19 campuses, ranging from Harvard to San Diego State. They divided the professors into two groups, those with a right-wing party affiliation (such as Republican or Libertarian) and those with a left-wing affiliation (such as Democrat or Communist). The results were consistent with their earlier findings: At Brown, the ratio of left to right was 18:1; at the University of

Colorado, it was 23:1. At UCLA, the liberal dominance was 16:1, while Syracuse University logged in at 25:1.

In 2001, Princeton Survey Research Associates International delivered a questionnaire to a sample of political scientists, historians, economists, and sociologists, inquiring whether they felt the government should be involved in 50 different areas of life. These Ph.D.'s (Democrats by a ratio of 9:1) felt that it was "important" for the government to expand its role in all 50 areas. This finding is consonant with the 1999 North American Academic Study Survey of 183 colleges, which found faculty routinely agreeing with all liberal causes, and feeling that the government should actively reduce the gaps in income, ensure full employment, and protect the environment despite costs to jobs and the economy.

In 2002, the Center for the Study of Popular Culture examined voter registration among the liberal arts departments at 32 elite colleges and universities. They found that Democrats outnumbered Republicans by a margin of 10:1.

A 2004 survey by *The Chronicle of Higher Education* found that 51 percent of Americans believed that faculty "improperly introduce a liberal bias in what they teach."

A 2004 survey by the Center for Survey Research and Analysis was sent to students at the 50 top-ranked colleges and universities rated by *U.S. News & World Report.* Some 49 percent of the students reported that professors routinely injected gratuitous political commentary into their classes. Nearly one-third (29 percent) felt that they had to agree with a professor's political views in order to get a good grade. In a 2005 study by the American Council of Trustees and Alumni (ACTA), 29 percent of students similarly reported that they felt they had to agree with the professors' political or social views to get a good grade.

This is reminiscent of the brainwashing techniques practiced by the Chinese Communists during the Korean War on U.S. prisoners of war. The captives were made to read anti-U.S. propaganda and then write essays discussing it. Prisoners who included any (even mildly) negative comments about our country were rewarded with cigarettes and the like. They also found that any passages they wrote that were critical of our country were read over the camp's loudspeakers, with full attribution. Then the same process would be repeated.

Tactics like these were astonishingly successful in turning them against their native land, at least temporarily. Today this same basic methodology is practiced not in Communist POW camps, but on American campuses. Thus, a final exam at the University of Northern Colorado contained the following required essay: "Make the argument that the military action of the U.S. attacking Iraq was criminal." If the professor had stated instead, "Make the argument that killing an unborn fetus is criminal," the ACLU would have put his brain in a jar for reprogramming.

The Center for Survey Research and Analysis study was conducted just before the 2004 Presidential election, and 68 percent of students reported hearing negative remarks about President Bush, while 62 percent reported that their professors praised Senator Kerry. Along the same lines, the University of California–Berkeley and Harvard ranked first and second in per capita employee contributions to the 2004 Kerry campaign, with Senator Kerry garnering $19 in support for every $1 donated to President Bush.

Stanley Rothman, S. Robert Lichter, and Neil Nevitte, writing in *The Forum* ("Politics and Professional Advancement Among College Faculty," Vol. 3: Issue

1, 2005), found that political ideology was the second most powerful predictor (after scholarly achievement) of the quality of the institution at which professors teach. Interestingly, being a practicing Christian was negatively related to quality of institutional affiliation. As they wrote: "When the logic of testing for differential outcomes according to race, gender, ethnicity, and sexual orientation is applied to ideology and religion, being a conservative, a Republican, or a practicing Christian confers a disadvantage in professional advancement greater than any of these other factors." The authors go on to note that "political conservatives have become an endangered species in some departments."

A review of recent trends also reveals:

- Academe has become far more liberal over time.

- Younger faculty are more liberal than older faculty.

- Liberals are more prevalent at the trend-setting "elite" colleges and universities.

- Disciplines cut off from objective standards are dramatically more liberal than disciplines where the scientific method prevails.

As *The Economist* wrote in 2004 ("America's One-Party State," 12/4, p. 36): "Academia is simultaneously both the part of America that is most obsessed with diversity, and the least diverse part of the country." Campus diversity officers make sure that minority, gay, lesbian, bisexual, and transgendered students are all welcome. But just as Henry Ford allowed customers to buy any color of Model T they wanted as long as it was black, there's diversity of thought only insofar as your thinking runs on liberal rails.

This leads to a hothouse of predictable group dynamics:

- *Groupthink,* where everybody thinks the same way and dissent is suppressed

- *Response polarization,* where issues are seen in black or white terms

- *A risky shift,* the lynch-mob effect

This all affects faculty decisions, as cowards hiding behind the shield of numeric invincibility goad each other to even more extreme positions than they would otherwise.

In other words, you have the high-toned U.S. liberal arts college of today. Even though this Orwellian thought control is antithetical to classical liberal ideas (remember the "free speech" movement of the 1960s?), the likelihood of change is nonexistent. Liberals aren't going to cede one of the few citadels where their ideas are taken seriously (among each other), even if it means sacrificing their principles to hold it.

Meanwhile, basic education is neglected. For all the twaddle about multiculturalism, only 10 percent of young adults in the U.S. can find Afghanistan on a map, according to *National Geographic*. Half can't even find New York.

Don't Know Much about History

Think of this country as a magnificent structure of human intelligence. It's founded first of all upon the Constitution, the greatest work of man's intellect of all time. Then it's based upon the laws of this country, which are founded upon all of humankind's experience in trying to apply some modicum of justice, order, and fairness to the incredibly confused dealings of hundreds of millions of men and women. To create a body of laws as fine as ours, based upon a Constitution as perfect as ours, took millennia of accumulated knowledge, reaching from ancient times forward to find what worked to secure freedom and order at once. In other words, it required a knowledge of history. It took *Homo sapiens* many years to reach the Enlightenment, and still more years to create America. During all of that time, man was building up an immense capital in his knowledge of history.

Upon this knowledge was the great edifice of our nation founded. There couldn't have been an America without a deep understanding of history. That capital continued to grow after the country began. It's evident from the documents written by Americans of the 19th century—even ordinary soldiers in the Civil War—that they were familiar with ancient and medieval history, and the modern history of their times.

Yet today, history has simply stopped being taught or understood in any sensible way. To preserve America, there has to be an appreciation of just how rare and precious a nation founded upon consent of the governed is, let alone one where that consent is rapidly extended even to persons previously considered to be only property. Young people have to know that through most of man's existence, societies were organized for the few to exploit the many. Young people—and all people—have to know that daily life in the past in nearly all times and places was based upon keeping the masses in submission with violence and dogma, wringing what could be wrung out of them, and using them for any purpose that suited the masters of the society, including killing them.

If young people don't understand that this changed only slowly and with great sacrifice, first in England and then in America, and that we are a stark departure from the way society operated in the past, the younger generations won't value America the way they should. If they don't understand that the "great" political revolutions of the modern era, Communism and Fascism, were based upon the subjugation of the tens of millions to allow the supremacy of the few, or even the one, with human life held to be of no value, they won't be willing to make the efforts necessary to guard this society for generations hence. To put it bluntly, if everyone doesn't understand just how much of a gem America is, we can lose America.

In spite of this, many young Americans simply know almost no history at all. They have no idea how the Roman Empire worked, and they know little or nothing about how the Aztec world operated. They know almost zilch about how Stalin ran the Soviet Union or how the modern Communist Chinese state—workplace of the world—was born in an orgy of mass murder. To see how far we've sunk, consider the following essay questions required of applicants to the University of Washington in 1908:

Ancient History
(Choose any eight of the following)

1. Describe an Egyptian temple.

2. Compare the early history of Babylonia with that of Egypt.

3. What is an oligarchy?

4. What did Solon do for Athens?

5. Describe slavery in Athens.

6. What causes contributed to Alexander's victories?

7. What was the tribune in early Rome?

8. What was the Roman phalanx?

9. What did Caesar do for Rome?

10. What was the praetorian guard?

Mediaeval and Modern History
(Choose any eight of the following)

1. Compare the empire of Otto I with that of Charlemagne.

2. Would the Pope have acquired temporal power if Rome had continued to be the residence of an Emperor?

3. Who were the Minnesingers?

4. What were the guilds?

5. What is meant by the Hundred Years' War?

6. Describe the Battle of Crécy.

7. Who was Richelieu?

8. What was the Holy Alliance?

9. What caused the Crimean war?

10. Give some of the results of the war between Russia and Japan in 1904–1905.

English History

(Choose any eight of the following)

1. How did Pope Gregory become interested in the conversion of England?

2. Why did William I curtail the power of his barons?

3. What were the early forest laws?

4. What was "mortmain" (a dead hand) in early English history?

5. Why was King Henry VIII popular?

6. How did England meet Spain's Invincible Armada?

7. Name the Stuart kings of England.

8. What was Robert Walpole's greatest contribution to English history?

9. What was the pocket-borough system?

10. How did Queen Victoria also become Empress of India?

American History
(Choose any eight of the following)

1. Name the great drainage systems of the United States.

2. What European countries had colonies in North America in 1750?

3. What were the limits of the United States in 1783; in 1804; in 1820?

4. What were the Virginia and Kentucky resolutions?

5. What was nullification?

6. What was secession?

7. Give dates of the beginning and ending of the war between the states.

8. What was the fifteenth amendment to the Constitution?

9. What was the Trent Affair?

10. How was the Hayes-Tilden election contest settled?

In other words, these are the topics that the college-bound high school grad in 1907 would be expected to know. It seems questionable whether the teaching of history has advanced in the intervening century. In fact, based on what we see, few of today's history doctoral students could pass this exam.

Instead, students today are often taught that Marxism, author of more misery than any other system in man's history, is a legitimate if not superior way to organize society. They're taught that state ownership is a legitimate way to eliminate racism and gender bias, instead of being just another way to facilitate the domination of the many by the few. They're taught that our own society is a cesspool of racism, oppression, and colonialism. If anyone should happen to be so out of step as to praise America, that is condemned as "triumphalism" and "exceptionalism."

College courses teach about the grievances of interest groups, racial groups, and gender groups. They detail how America and Europe got rich by exploitation. But very little is taught about how the American Revolution was and is the light of human freedom across the world. Little is taught about how the free-market economy is the primary engine for prosperity all across the world, and how America was the first great example of it on a continental basis. Students are taught about America's record of racism, but they are rarely taught that close to 400,000 American white men gave their lives to win a struggle that freed the slaves, and how this was unprecedented in human history. They're largely unaware that America rescued all of western Europe after World War II, only to have much of it turn hostile to us, or that we rebuilt Japan and didn't ask for one penny of reparations. If they even hear of reparations at all, it's in the context of the demand by politicians for reparations for slavery.

Do we exaggerate? Let's open the catalog from that elite, trendsetting Ivy League school Brown University, and see the listings for the fall of 2007. It lists 18 courses offered in the area of gender and sexuality studies, and no fewer than 90 courses offered in African studies. But suppose our tastes run to, say, American history. What is Brown plating up for its students regarding the Civil War?

- **Body and Soul: Health and Sexuality, 1860–1920** examines "the history of women/gender in relation to discourses about sexuality (both physical and mental) in the era of the Civil War."

- **Antebellum America and the Road to the Civil War** teaches us about the social order of slavery.

- **The Old South and Slavery** teaches about slavery and the Old South.

Lest we skim over this topic, there's also **Comparative American Slavery** and another course titled **Slavery in American History, Culture and Memory**, which demonstrates that far from being a practice that ended 140-plus years ago, "slavery remains a palpable presence in the United States."

- **Civil War and Reconstruction**, with special emphasis on slavery and emancipation. "Not a course on military history," it hastens to add. A gratuitous add-on, since we failed to find a single course on military history anywhere in Brown's catalog. Thank God we live in a world where war has been made irrelevant by peace-loving academics.

But wait! There's more:

- **American Cultural History, 1789–1865:** " . . . the course focuses on American slavery and draws on Southern legal documents to consider how enslaved men and women contested the commodification, medicalization, criminalization, and sexualization of their bodies."

But to really get at the pith and marrow of America, we recommend:

- **Introduction to American Studies,** which will focus on "for example, a neighborhood, an ethnic group, an event—and examine them in depth through history, fiction, film, and other media." We only hope they don't overlook discussing TV commercials in this challenging offering.

Looking further afield, we were disappointed with the **History of Sexuality in the United States.** The class description, which says that the course "introduces students to the history of sexuality in America from the colonial era to the present," goes on to add: "[t]his is not only a history of gay and lesbian communities." Well, why not? Aren't gays and lesbians deserving of a course all their own? Frankly, we detect a whiff of crypto-homophobia here.

Not to point fingers, but we couldn't help noticing that Brown offers a course on **The Black Female Body in American Culture,** yet overlooks providing any equivalent offering on white, Latina, or Asian female bodies. Fortunately, **American Masculinities** helps students explore what it means to "be a man" (which they put in quotes), while those tired female stereotypes go the way of the whalebone corset in **U.S. Feminist Theories of Motherhood,** in which we learn that motherhood is a social construct.

What Happened?

Like everything else, it's all Nixon's fault. Cognitive dissonance forced college kids in the 1960s to become radicals in order to (over) justify their not wanting to serve in Vietnam. Many ducked the draft by staying in school and stuck around the coffee shop long enough to be issued Ph.D.'s. That led naturally enough to a career in the cozy cocoon of college. Since their beliefs were never tested in the real world (school was the only environment they had known), they never outgrew them. Instead, they lucked into a niche in the one area of the world where they could spout off and others (impressionable young students even more ignorant than they) would be forced to listen. In this superoxygenated environment, their egos began expanding exponentially.

Soon, the university became a straitjacket that provided insufficient scope for these professors' egos and their need to feel relevant and important. No longer content with merely teaching their assigned subject areas, they transformed the university from an ivied ivory tower into a catalyst for social change. This meant discarding the old notion of the university as a haven for the disinterested pursuit of knowledge, and substituting a passionate political agenda of their own choosing—a new order where they'd be on top because they had all the answers.

By this point they had punched the clock long enough to have tenure, so there was no stopping them—at least on campus. The outside world barely noticed, except on occasion when something completely ridiculous happened, and it crashed into the newspapers.

Communist professor Herbert Marcuse at Brandeis wrote an essay on "Repressive Tolerance" in 1965, which had provided an explicit justification for denying conservatives the right to equal time, on the grounds that a balanced intellectual platform furthered the conservative agenda all by itself. It wasn't long before conservative professors were excluded from hiring committees and campus speeches, while radicals were imported at every opportunity. The tenor of campus life changed, and more moderate and conservative professors didn't want to be heckled or accused of being Uncle Toms. But the trade-off is that they became "good Germans" who looked the other way while the nonpartisan basis of the university was destroyed.

The next step was the creation of whole departments to further political causes with barely any scholarly pretense to cover their purpose: Black Studies; Feminist Studies; Cultural Studies; Peace Studies; Social Justice Studies; Gay, Lesbian, Transgendered, Questioning, and Bi-Curious Studies . . . and so on. It wasn't long before these programs went interdisciplinary and established beachheads in ordinary departments such as English and History, eviscerating scholarly standards wherever they landed.

As David Horowitz (to whom we're much indebted) calculates in his excellent work *The Professors: The 101 Most Dangerous Academics in America,* the total number of college and university professors in the United States is 617,000. If we very conservatively assume that roughly 5 percent per university faculty are radicals, then the total number of such professors at American universities might be 30,000, and the number of students annually passing through their classrooms would be of the order of 100 times that, or three million. These are America's sons and daughters, going to college to attain "excellences of the head" and coming out with heads of cabbage.

What are they learning?

- According to Professors Barash and Webel (authors of *Peace and Conflict Studies,* an $87.95 textbook used in more than 250 Peace Studies programs), the American founding fathers were terrorists, while the terrorists in Iraq are patriots.

- At the University of California–Davis, a professor told the class that the number one terrorist in the Middle East was Jesus Christ.

- At the University of Illinois–Chicago, Distinguished Professor of Education, Senior University Scholar, and Communist William Ayers expressed regret that the terrorists "didn't bomb enough."

- Even mathematics has become fair game for social justice, with *Rethinking Mathematics: Teaching Social Justice by the*

Numbers (Eric Gutstein and Bob Peterson, eds.) now a leading text. As one reviewer enthusiastically notes: "This book shows how teachers who are dedicated to social justice can act on their commitments in a subject that has, for too long, been seen as simply a technical area." This reminds us of nothing so much as the Nazi textbooks, which were salted with problems like this: "The Jews are aliens in Germany—in 1933 there were 66,060,000 inhabitants in the German Reich, of whom 499,682 were Jews. What is the percent of aliens?"

- At the University of Colorado, Professor Ward Churchill characterized the victims of 9/11 as "little Eichmanns," since America is a genocidal nation run by international criminals. A subsequent examination of his bogus academic record led to his dismissal, fortunately.

- Duke University students were treated to a rousing talk by Weather Underground member Laura Whitehorn, who was invited as an official guest of the school's African American Studies department. Her only peccadillo was plotting to bomb the U.S. Capitol building, which led to 14 years in prison. If you missed her at Duke, you can probably catch her elsewhere: She has also spoken at Brown, Vassar, Cornell, and the like.

- Unfortunately, Susan Rosenberg has decided to withdraw from the offer to be a visiting professor at Hamilton College. Her 16-year stint in prison for possession of 600 pounds of explosives as a member of the Weather Underground caused a stir; this class will have to be rescheduled. Luckily for Rosenberg, she has friends in high places: She was one of the 139 freed or given commuted sentences by President Clinton in his final hours in office.

But nothing sums up the state of academe today quite so well as Larry Summers's firing as Harvard's president. Summers first got into trouble by attempting to get African-American studies professor and hip-hop singer Cornel West to produce some scholarly work befitting a Harvard professor. West responded by claiming that Summers had "disrespected" him and the entire African-American community at Harvard. Summers backed down and apologized, but West was unmollified and eventually decamped for Princeton, once a great university.

Next, Summers addressed a symposium where he raised the question of why there weren't more women at the highest levels of science (such as tenured professors), citing empirical data on the topic. He wondered if it might be genetic, saying that wasn't his view. A female professor in attendance walked out (fearing if she stayed she would have "blacked out or thrown up") and called the newspaper; calls for Summers's resignation quickly followed. He apologized and sought to clarify that he meant no disrespect to women or to imply anything about their scientific aptitude. However, the subject was closed for discussion. The faculty pulled the plug and Summers was removed, the distinguished economist and former secretary of the treasury reduced to an object lesson on what happens to any administrator who dares to tangle with campus radicals.

Summary

Something very strange has happened at the highest reaches of education. It's as if aliens had landed and taken over the universities, replacing sensible professors and responsible administrators with complete screwballs. Can we expect students trained at these institutions to be able to compete for the jobs of tomorrow on the global stage with the high IQ, workaholic Indian, Chinese, Japanese, and Korean students? (Never mind that on standardized tests, American high school students now score on a par with students from the Slovak Republic in science, while their math scores are slightly below those of kids from Azerbaijan.) Many of those who survive high school will be ghettoized by foolish and cowardly professors who pander to their students instead of giving them the education they need and deserve.

There's a wild disconnect between what's happening in America and what young people are learning about it. This country is becoming more free, more open, more than ever the land of opportunity. Americans are working together better than ever before. At the same time, universities are saying that this is a hopelessly flawed, racist, exploitative, and homophobic state and that young people—already raised on massive doses of vapid self-esteem in the post-Spock era—are in fact victims and dupes of the same machinery that gave us warmongering and slavery and Halliburton and global warming. There's a surreal disconnect between town and gown.

Young people are being instructed in "anti-history"—a history that falsely teaches that America is more blameworthy than praiseworthy. This attacks the basic foundation of society by telling students that their identities are mere social conventions, and that above all else, they're victims. It's difficult to envision how educated classes who are taught that motherhood and masculinity are just arbitrary social constructs are going to constitute a home of the brave that will be willing to fight to keep it the land of the free. It is all too easy to imagine how such a society will rot from within.

Perhaps the sight of how well America works day by day will erase the nonsense that young people are taught in school, and this will be sufficient to rebuild the human capital needed to keep the society strong. The future needs far more appreciation of America. The record of the accomplishments of human dignity and opportunity is so shining that it has to be taught, not ignored or ridiculed in fashionable "academese." If

America is to last as long as it deserves to, if it is to keep flowering, then the next 75 years need to showcase more praise of what has gone right and less whining about what, in the story of America, are just tiny eddies in an onrushing river of human progress.

We are still the shining "city upon a hill" (as early Ronald Reagan speechwriter John Winthrop penned in 1630), a great country in its great days—but for how long? Not long if too many academics have their way.

✷   ✷   ✷

Chapter Three

Debase
American Culture

☆ ☆

May 2007 Gallup Poll

Q: Right now, do you think the state of moral values in the country is getting better or getting worse?

Better	Worse
11%	82%

An extremely shrewd move toward ruining the United States of America will be to weaken the culture to a point where it's outwardly smug and self-congratulatory, while inwardly navel-gazing and crippled with self-doubt. Then add a laugh track or a pounding rock beat so that everything feels good all the time. Finish with a hefty swig from the River Lethe to erase any collective knowledge of America's historical stature such that people will remain completely docile and unaware that anything of value has been lost.

In the last chapter, we saw how Gramsci's plan to undermine the West from within has been successfully implemented in academe. Here, we'll discover that it has gathered a solid foundation in the rest of our country's cultural institutions as well. We're especially indebted in this survey to Brent Bozell's Culture and Media Institute for tracking this exchange of bread and circuses for traditional values in today's giant reality show of American life.

The decline of moral values has not completely escaped notice. To quote from Gallup once again:

May 2007 Gallup Poll

Q: How would you rate the overall state of moral values in this country today—as excellent, good, only fair, or poor?

Excellent	Good	Only fair	Poor
1	16	39	44

In the National Cultural Values Survey of 2,000 Americans conducted by the polling firm of Fabrizio, McLaughlin & Associates for the Culture and Media Institute, 74 percent of Americans believe that moral values in America are weaker than they were 20 years ago. Nearly half said that morals were "much weaker." The survey found that 68 percent of Americans, including majorities in every demographic group sampled, believe the media are contributing to moral decline. The conclusions were supported by Republicans, Democrats, liberals, conservatives, Christians, Jews, and secularists.

The Decline of Post-War Culture

Let's look at a few prizes from the post–World War II period and from recent times.

Pulitzer Prizes

Back then:

1940 – *The Grapes of Wrath*
1944 – *Oklahoma!*
1947 – *All the King's Men*
1948 – *A Streetcar Named Desire*
1949 – *Death of a Salesman*
1950 – *South Pacific*
1952 – *The Caine Mutiny*
1953 – *The Old Man and the Sea*
1955 – *Cat on a Hot Tin Roof*

. . . and more recently:

1999 – *The Hours*
2000 – *Interpreter of Maladies*
2001 – *The Amazing Adventures of Kavalier & Clay*
2002 – *Empire Falls*
2003 – *Middlesex*
2004 – *The Known World*
2005 – *Gilead*
2006 – *March*
2007 – *The Road*

So much for the Pulitzers. Let's tee up some Nobels.

Nobel Prizes for Literature

Back then:

1946 – Hermann Hesse
1947 – André Gide
1948 – T. S. Eliot
1949 – William Faulkner
1950 – Bertrand Russell

. . . and now:

2002 – Imre Kertész
2003 – J. M. Coetzee
2004 – Elfriede Jelinek
2005 – Harold Pinter
2006 – Orhan Pamuk

You've probably heard of the household names from the immediate postwar period—you may have even read some of them. But the recent list is relatively unknown to those of us who don't teach postmodern literature at Mount Holyoke. These are writers and works that have passed from obscurity straight to the remainder pile without going through any intervening stage of general readership. We suspect that the post-war writers were more readable and wrote for a more broadly educated population of readers, rather than for the delectation of English professors. That is highbrow lit today.

It's hard to believe the general collapse of modern popular culture that has taken place in the interven-ing period. The Supreme Court basically said that any-thing goes if you call it free speech, and then out went a decent culture. The effects this has on young Americans are horrifying.

Today, adolescents dominate the media. They're the main consumers of mass culture. With their short attention spans, demand for painless and stress-free lives, need to blame everyone else for their problems, and perpetual sense of victimization, adolescents are the model for the whole society. As a result, our mass culture is too cool for school and instead promotes drug use, sex, and violence. As kids learn to be stupid instead of smart, the national intelligence needed to compete in the global economy of the 21st century will simply vanish into MTV-land, and the moral superiority to defeat Islamic terrorism will be gone.

Hollywood

"When I go to see an R-rated horror movie, I want lots of violence. I want nudity. I want sex and violence mixed together. What's wrong with that? . . . We're in a really violent wave [of horror movies] and I hope it never ends. Hopefully we'll get to a point where there are absolutely no restrictions on any kind of violence in movies."
— **Eli Roth,** horror-movie director

Once again, let's compare the output of the postwar period in Hollywood with that of today.

Academy Award Winners in Major Categories

Back then:

1945 – *The Lost Weekend, Mildred Pierce, National Velvet, The Bells of St. Mary's*

1946 – *The Best Years of Our Lives*

1947 – *Miracle on 34th Street, Gentleman's Agreement, The Bishop's Wife*

1948 – *Hamlet, Key Largo, The Treasure of the Sierra Madre*

1949 – *All the King's Men, The Heiress, Little Women*

1950 – *Harvey, All About Eve, Cyrano De Bergerac, The Third Man, Sunset Boulevard*

1951 – *The African Queen, A Streetcar Named Desire, An American in Paris, A Place in the Sun*

1952 – *High Noon; Come Back, Little Sheba*

1953 – *Stalag 17, From Here to Eternity, Roman Holiday*

1954 – *On the Waterfront, Sabrina*

1955 – *Marty, Mister Roberts, To Catch a Thief, Picnic, Oklahoma!*

Today:

1999 – *American Beauty, The Cider House Rules*

2000 – *Traffic, Gladiator, Erin Brockovich*

2001 – *A Beautiful Mind, Training Day, The Lord of the Rings: The Fellowship of the Ring*

2002 – *Chicago, The Pianist, Bowling for Columbine*

2003 – *The Lord of the Rings: The Return of the King, Cold Mountain, Mystic River*

2004 – *Ray, Million Dollar Baby*

2005 – *Crash, Brokeback Mountain, Capote*

2006 – *The Departed, An Inconvenient Truth,
Pan's Labyrinth*

What's completely inescapable is the stunning fall in quality and what might be called a generalized hatred of America.

When Hollywood started, it was run by Jewish immigrants who were on their hands and knees, grateful to be in America rather than in the horrible, pogrom-ridden villages of Russia. We got super-patriotic movies like *Over There* and *Wings.* We saw reverent depictions of small-town America, such as *It's a Wonderful Life,* because it was something they admired; and America was a place where they wanted to be accepted.

Then, cranks and crackpots came out west to be writers. They were malcontents and complainers, Communists and fellow travelers, who (like some modern academics) were secure enough to hate America. They created the anti-American ethos of contempt for the military, for small towns, and for family life that stays with us even to this day. Hollywood is a hotbed of discontent even amidst staggering plenty and prosperity—a spoiled, pampered, but sullen and fault-finding teenager. Worse, it acts this way while exploding with moral pretentiousness.

Interestingly, while Hollywood has done many movies and TV shows about the horrible crimes of the Nazis, and even a few about the grisly atrocities of the Japanese, Hollywood has never—not once—made a movie or documentary about the whole terrible tragedy of Soviet Communism: the mass murders by Lenin and the Reds, the bloody purges by Stalin, the murder of entire classes of people, the nation's transformation into a terrorized "cattle car" of informants and victims.

Why is there no *Schindler's List* about the enforced starvation of the brave Ukrainian people, who were so deprived of their own food grown in their own fields that they resorted to cannibalism? Why is there no *Shoah* of the gulag? Communism made the largest nation in the world in geography and the third biggest (once) in population into a vast torture chamber and graveyard. All this was going on well into the 1950s.

How does Hollywood respond? At a *Rolling Stone* photo shoot, Johnny Depp wore a "Che" Guevara pendant. Depp has proclaimed his "digging" of the Communist revolutionary. What a wonderful hero to have. Cuba is practically one vast concentration camp. Meanwhile, as John Meroney pointed out in the *National Review,* Communist filmmakers such as Dalton

Trumbo; Ring Lardner, Jr.; and Paul Jarrico are regarded as courageous pioneers even to this day, while the anti-Communist screenwriters like Morrie Ryskind, James McGuinness, and Martin Berkeley have been ridden out of town, and Ronald Reagan's Hollywood career is treated as a joke.

Why has Hollywood never dealt with this? What is the attraction of this evil system for Hollywood and for "intellectuals" generally that keeps them from facing the truth about how vicious Communism was and is? Why would Hollywood, a place for creative individuals and bad boys, like Communism, a machine for making people soulless and conformist? Why would Jews in Hollywood—who should know what happens to Jews in totalitarian systems—forgive Communism so utterly? Why do they ignore or minimize the most horrific misconduct imaginable by left-wing regimes while focusing an electron microscope on the "evils" of the United States?

If Americans got all of their information about the world and the 20th century from the mass culture, they'd assume that there were a number of evils in the past hundred years: big business, big business, big business, medium-sized business, small business, American racism, environmental pollution, and the oppression of women and homosexuals. But they would know nothing about the Communist evil that has claimed the lives of more than 100 million innocent men, women, and children in Russia, China, Eastern Europe, Southeast Asia, Cuba, and elsewhere.

Even today, when we're at war with Islamic terrorism, there's almost nothing shown about how horrifying life is in repressive Islamic regimes. There are movies about gangsters, drug dealers, and the Ku Klux Klan, and there should be. But where are movies about the staggering repression of human beings in fundamentalist Islamic societies? They don't exist, because it might hurt our enemies' feelings to be portrayed exactly as they are.

Instead, what do we see? Hollywood is interested in breaking the taboos that ordinary middle-class people respect. For example, at the trendsetting Sundance Film Festival in 2007, the film *Zoo* chronicled the daring exploits of a group of Seattle men who like to have sex with horses. Just when you think things can't get any worse, they can.

Television

> *"This Easter, take off your Sunday best,
> and turn on your favorite shows."*

— ABC promotional voice-over playing as
Desperate Housewives' Nicollette Sheridan peels
off her blouse on Christianity's holiest day

Prime-time network television has declined from Newton Minow's vast wasteland of the mid-20th century to a full-on trailer park of trash talk, sex, and violence today, lowering the quality of life for all Americans in the process.

According to the Parents Television Council, not only is prime-time network television more violent than ever before, much of the violence is increasingly of a sexual nature. Depictions of violence are up 75 percent since 1998, and it's shown far more graphically. Murder, rape, and assault are standard fare, wall to wall throughout prime time. The frequency of violence in adult programming—4.41 incidents per hour—is surpassed by the portrayal of violence in children's programming, where cartoons and children's shows evidenced an average of more than 6 instances of violence per hour. A study by the Parents Television Council found violence, bad language, sexual content, and rebellion throughout even the Nickelodeon network's programming.

As virtually every study on the topic has confirmed since the surgeon general's original report in 1972, watching television violence correlates with an increase in aggressive behavior in children. On this point, the American Psychological Association, the American Medical Association, and the American Academy of Pediatrics all agree. Deborah A. Fisher, Ph.D., of the Pacific Institute for Research and Evaluation, estimates that children are typically exposed to 1,000 murders, rapes, and assaults per year from their television viewing. She warns that early exposure to television violence is a consistent and significant predictor of later aggressive behavior. Beyond the psychological effects of being immersed in so much violence—such as increased fear, anxiety, obsessive thoughts, and sleep disturbances— this subject matter also serves to desensitize children to violence in the outside world. The net effect is that they become less empathetic with victims of violence and less inclined to help them.

If all this weren't bad enough, the National Cultural Values Survey commissioned by the Culture and Media

Institute shows a correlation between high television exposure and lax morals. People who watch four or more hours of television daily are less committed to honesty and charity and are more permissive about sex and abortion. On the other hand, people who watch one hour or less per evening are more likely to attend religious services and attempt to live according to God's commandments. Among the findings are these statistics:

- Heavy television viewers have a passive "do me something" attitude compared with light viewers, expecting government to provide for their retirements (64 percent to 43 percent) and health care (63 percent to 48 percent).

- Light viewers are more likely than heavy viewers to contribute their time or treasure to charitable causes. In fact, heavy viewers are more than twice as likely to give nothing at all (24 percent to 11 percent) and not to volunteer (56 percent to 27 percent).

- Is sex outside of marriage wrong? Yes, say 39 percent of light viewers, while only 26 percent of heavy viewers concur.

Special censure should be held out for MTV in this regard. It's not too much of a stretch to suggest, as does Kristen Fyfe of the Culture and Media Institute, that MTV has contributed more to the death of innocence and the early sexualization of children than any other media outlet, forcing children into roles for which they aren't mentally, physically, or emotionally prepared. According to Fyfe: "MTV broadcasts hours upon hours of highly sexualized videos, obscene language and celebrations of sex, drug use, drinking and in-your-face defiance of authority. Shows like *Real World, Spring Break* and *Wild Girls of Makos* highlight debauchery day in and day out."

Time magazine reports that girls aged 7 to 12 spend $1.6 million on thong underwear. Before outraged parents protested and stopped them, Hasbro put out a line of dolls based on the Pussycat Dolls, musical tramps known for their explicit lyrics and dance routines

Music

Truly, if a man from outer space observed our culture today and then looked at culture in the postwar period, he would faint at how we've gone backward.

We used to have Ricky Nelson, Pat Boone, and the young Elvis Presley on the pop charts, singing about young love, drive-ins, and the malt shop; and now our young people listen to songs glorifying rape, drug use, and the murder of strangers. This is not a matter of black versus white performers—think of Count Basie and any song penned by Chuck Berry. There was once a time when culture assumed gentleness on the part of the nation. Now it assumes "Thug Nation."

Think for a minute of some of the songs you know from the 1940s:

- "You Made Me Love You"
- "When You Wish Upon a Star"
- "White Christmas"
- "Some Enchanted Evening"

The list of great songs from the postwar decades is nearly endless. Now compare that with today's rap music. The amount of violence, profanity, misogyny, vulgarity, and perversion in rap and hip-hop lyrics is stunning. First, there is the stupefying use of "the n word," which supposedly causes irreparable anguish when uttered by a white person but which peppers rap in almost every verse. This has an unfortunate consequence, as white suburban teenagers who are one of rap's principal audiences now routinely refer to blacks in that way. This is not a step forward. Rather, it is a stunning betrayal of the civil-rights movement and the sacrifices of Dr. Martin Luther King, Jr.; Medgar Evers; Andrew Goodman; James Earl Chaney; Michael Schwerner; and too many others.

Second, rap is staggeringly antiwoman. It amazes us that the women's-rights lobby is too busy fighting for abortion and for allowing multimillionaire females into country clubs to notice that the most popular musical form among youth today routinely refers to nearly all women as "hos" and "bitches." Don Imus can't get away with this—why is it tolerated on the rest of the radio dial?

The standard seems to be to use women for sex, beat them up, make them work as prostitutes, breed them—but never show them any respect unless they're good singers. There are continual references to killing women, cutting their throats, strangling them, beating them if they don't turn over their money—and it's breathtakingly antisocial and antihuman.

Years ago, the Rand Corporation released a study finding that heavy exposure to sexual content on television shows correlated strongly with teenagers' initiation of sexual intercourse. Then, in August 2006, they published a new study in the journal *Pediatrics* on the subject of teenagers and music. Based on interviews with nearly 1,500 teens, those who listened to sexually explicit music were almost twice as likely to start having sex within the following two years than those who didn't. This finding held for boys and girls, and for whites and nonwhites—even after accounting for a list of other personal and social factors associated with adolescent sexual behavior.

Adolescents typically listen to 1.5 to 2.5 hours of music per day, and this doesn't include the time they spend watching music videos. While allusions to sex have always been found in popular music, today's lyrics dispense with euphemism, metaphor, and double entendre, let alone wit or nuance. Rap artist Lil' Kim's songs are typical, and include such classics as "F--- You," "Shut up B---h," and "Suck my D--k."

Airhead Nation

A broad sampling of popular culture today reveals the following:

— **The sociopath is a hero.** Today's Hollywood hero is a man with no ties or attachments to anything. Even if he works as a police officer, he has contempt for authority as well as ordinary working stiffs. Rules that apply to others don't apply to him. With a smart mouth and a slick manner, charming when he wants to be but explosively violent just beneath the surface, he has sex with any girl he wants, but soon she'll end up dead or forgotten. He solves problems with a gun. We can't recall a time when a serious personality disorder would be held up as a role model or hero for a generation.

— **Saving and thrift are contemptible.** People in their 20s are typically portrayed as driving $100,000 automobiles, living in million-dollar-decorated apartments, vacationing in Bali, and hanging out with others of similar ilk. A high-consumption lifestyle is the norm, and the message is clear: Don't bother to save any money. That's for people who don't know how to enjoy life right here and now—in other words, losers. You're always going to have a great job, score big on the stock market, or have "friends" you can take advantage of. There won't be any rainy days in your life. Better to live for today, and when tomorrow comes, live for today then as well. No reason to scrimp today when you can liquidate assets like home equity and plow them into current consumption.

— **Family life is for squares.** Those folks are just a ball and chain on you anyway. Who needs 'em? Your parents? Screw 'em; they're boring old nags. Your kids? Just a drain. Your spouse? Just expects all the attention for him- or herself, when by all rights *you* should be getting all of the attention. In fact, the institution of marriage itself is just a dinosaur from the farm era before people really had options. Less than half of the women 15 and over are now living with a husband, according to the Census Bureau. There's no reason why children should have two parents, or even why anyone should have children at all. Let's have a culture where there are more abortions than births.

— **The other guy is always to blame for everything.** There's no need for any form of individual self-restraint or self-control. We're exempt from any responsibility for our own actions as long as there's someone around with deep pockets that we can rifle. We should punish tobacco companies on the theory that they compel innocent people to smoke. We should blame the restaurant that serves us fries, and shake down a drug company for our mistakes in self-medication.

— **Hard work is for suckers.** All true wealth comes from skillful manipulation and cunning or from finding some angle that leave the plodding, workaday Jane or Joe in the dust. Make sure that society's idols are men and women who got rich from being sexy in public or through gambling or playing tricks—not from hard work, patience, or self-discipline. This leaves everyone permanently envious and bewildered about where true success comes from.

— **Disrespect the law and the conventions of society in every possible way.** Make sure that uncouth manners and a slovenly appearance become normative. Just look out for numero uno. This will dissolve the glue that holds the nation together and dissuade any long-term thinking. Following the law or time-honored social conventions is for chumps.

— **Self-discipline and mastery of any field or skill can be achieved through fantasy instead of hard work.** A quick montage is all that it takes to acquire great expertise in any endeavor. Even easier, just take drugs to enhance your performance and pretty soon you'll be another Barry Bonds.

The Real Stars

Unbelievably, as we write this, the TV shows a spoiled heiress whimpering for her parents to save her as she's being hauled off to jail for her third drunk-driving offense. We can't help but wonder: Is this the attitude that's going to keep America strong and free?

As one of us (Ben Stein) wrote a few years ago:

> A man or woman is not a "star" if he gets paid tens of millions of dollars to say lines in front of a camera. She's not a "star" if she gets paid millions to simper and look sad because an imaginary boyfriend did not call. He's not a "star" if he gets paid thousands of dollars a minute to run up and down a wooden basketball court. They may be good actors and super great athletes, but in my mind, they're not stars. The real stars, the ones who keep this country free on Independence Day and every day, are the ones who lead a patrol down an alley in Falluja with some maniac terrorist aiming an AK-47 at their heads. The real stars are the ones who leave their families behind at a dusty Army base and go off and risk—and lose—their lives to do their duty by their country and free men and women everywhere.

With our country in the midst of a war with Islamic fundamentalists, the leading news story recently was the death of former Playmate Anna Nicole Smith, which received 691,000 news story mentions that week. Writing in *Human Events,* Gary Bauer recently tallied some recent celebrity mentions in the news media in a given week:

- Lindsay Lohan: 999
- Alex Rodriguez: 996
- Paris Hilton: 994
- Mahmoud Ahmadinejad: 301

While a certain amount of escapism is understandable, this suggests a country that has lost its moral compass and seriousness of purpose. Meanwhile, celebrities aren't satisfied with endless amounts of adulation, money, and sex—they also want to be morally superior. Thus U2's Bono entraps politicians into donating our money to failed aid programs, Scientology's Tom Cruise warns us of the dangers of modern psychiatry, and Rosie O'Donnell lectures about how apartheid in South Africa is similar to the United States under the Patriot Act and how radical Christianity is just as dangerous as radical Islam.

America the Beautiful: Forgotten

With the eradication of history and its replacement with America-bashing sloganeering, elementary truths once taken for granted throughout our society are perilously close to being forgotten. Consider: How long has it been since citizens began being the arbiters of their own government rather than used as chattel however rulers saw fit? How long has it been since men and women gained the ability to get rid of their leaders through ballots instead of revolution? Perhaps a few hundred years out of tens of thousands.

How long has man been able to have hot baths on demand? A century. How long has he been able to have safe, delicious food at any time? Maybe 80 or 100 years. How long has he been able to have an air-conditioned room in the desert? Fifty years. How long have Jews had completely equal rights with Christians in America? Perhaps 40 years at most, out of 5,800 years of Jewish life. How long have black men been in high political office in large numbers? Just 10 or 20 years. How long have women had completely equal rights?

In other words, America offers us a golden age on a silver salver—a life that's the envy of the world, a life of comfort, safety, health, and opportunity almost unimaginable to earlier generations.

Most of us have never been prisoners in a concentration camp. We've never been led into a gas chamber and gassed with Zyklon B. We've never been rounded up in a town in Romania and beaten to death by fascist thugs with iron rods. We've never been used for unanesthetized experiments by Dr. Mengele. We've never been on a death march in the Philippines. We've never gone hungry, never been forced to work outside in the Polish winter in cotton clothing while suffering from typhus. We haven't lived through an economic depression lasting 11 years, where our store of treasure turned to dust and able-bodied members of our family went hungry for lack of work. Yet these were the fates of millions, even in our lifetimes.

We never had to charge against massed cannon and musket fire in Fredericksburg, be a prisoner in a gulag, or be shot at the Lubyanka (intelligence headquarters) because some OGPU officer had to make his execution quota of "wreckers and saboteurs" in order to placate Stalin. We've never had to charge against German machine guns at Ypres or the Somme. We've never suffocated in the hold of a Japanese prison ship.

We've never had to charge against Japanese Nambu machine guns at Tarawa, Peleliu, or Okinawa. We have never been torpedoed while making the Murmansk run, then thrown overboard and drowned in icy water while our friends died all around us, or eaten by sharks because our ship was torpedoed in the Pacific by Japanese submarines.

How blessed most of us have been.

But the point of our thanks is that there are millions—tens of millions—who suffered and died to bring us the sunny pleasure dome that is America today. What's missing from our whole chocolatey-sweet culture is this realization of just how amazingly thankful we have to be to the men who died so that we could bitch and moan about traffic or bad cell-phone service. How will we ever be able to pay these people back? What can we do for the child without a grandfather because that man died assaulting Shuri Castle on Okinawa or defending Corregidor or breaking through to Bastogne or holding off the Chinese Communists at Chosin?

It seems as if the whole country is on the road to forgetting how we got to where we are. If we lose sight of just how precious our nation and our way of life are, we'll lose our purpose and our meaning, and we'll be easy prey for our enemies.

This has to be taught. We have everything we do because brave men bled and their wives, mothers, fathers, and children sobbed and were alone. This is what should be on TV—shows that bind the nation together in gratitude. But where do we start when women like Paris Hilton's mother are considered role models?

We aren't worried about America's financial capital. There's plenty of money and plenty of trinkets. We *are* worried about our moral capital. It's as if it has been loaded onto ships and is sailing out of sight. When it is gone, what will we do?

"Ye are the salt of the earth, but if the salt lose its savor, wherewith shall it be salted?"

Chapter Four

Weaken the United States Military

☆ ☆

Everyone knows that war isn't healthy for children and other living things. In order to ruin the United States of America, we think that the armed services can be shrunk to a point where we keep a few soldiers around to assist in disaster relief and march in Fourth-of-July parades. Peace will rule the planets. Defense spending should be pared and the proceeds distributed to more important government functions than defending our country.

Not everyone shares this view. Lieutenant General Michael D. Maples, director of the Defense Intelligence

Agency, has outlined a few minor problems facing our country in his address to the Senate Select Committee on Intelligence, as has J. Michael McConnell, director of National Intelligence, in his statement to the House Permanent Select Committee on Intelligence. In "This Friendly World," as Fabian sang, these are probably nothing that a little diplomacy can't smooth over. Perhaps with Bill Clinton as a roving ambassador, everything will be peaches and cream.

Let's take a quick tour of the globe.

Iraq

After 9/11, President George W. Bush had to make a bold response, and the invasion of Iraq became the centerpiece of his plan. Thanks to poltroonery and incompetence at the top of the CIA (George Tenet), the intelligence that got us involved in Iraq was deeply flawed but was nevertheless used to justify a war that some like Vice President Cheney and Deputy Secretary of Defense Paul Wolfowitz badly wanted at the time, to subdue the (nonexistent) threat from Saddam Hussein and to plant another flag of democracy in the Middle East (the other being Israel's). Colin Powell, the one man with misgivings and the moral authority to stop it, went along with the party line, even though he was no longer working as a general (where such obedience would be expected) but rather serving as the secretary of state.

After our soldiers quickly marched to Baghdad, the handling of the aftermath was disastrous. Secretary of Defense Rumsfeld woefully underestimated the numbers of troops necessary to secure the country, or possibly Bush and Rumsfeld felt that the best way to sell the war to America was to make it quick and painless. However, the lack of a meaningful plan for securing peace became readily apparent. Saddam's army was disbanded instead of redeployed, putting a million well-armed soldiers out of work. A rigorous campaign of "de-Ba'athification" then deprived all of the country's leaders of their jobs as well, allowing them to turn their attention to other causes.

After a protracted period while Bush and Rumsfeld fiddled while soldiers died, General Petraeus was finally put in charge, and troop levels were increased. As is well understood throughout the Islamic world, the American electorate quickly grows impatient with any war it isn't decisively winning and has little tolerance for a steady stream of casualties. As we go to press, it's uncertain whether Petraeus will be able to turn things around before the patience of the voters runs out, although signs are hopeful but not a sure thing.

Here was General Maples's description of the situation: "The perception of unchecked violence is creating an atmosphere of fear, hardening sectarianism, empowering militias and vigilante groups, hastening a middle-class exodus, and shaking confidence in government and security forces. The sectarian violence, a weak central government, problems in providing basic services, and high unemployment are encouraging more Iraqis to turn toward sectarian groups, militias, and insurgents for basic needs, threatening the unity of Iraq. Moreover, robust criminal networks act as insurgent and terrorist force multipliers. Many Sunni Arabs, motivated by fear, financial incentive, perceptions of marginalization, and exclusion from Iraqi government and security institutions, act as insurgent sympathizers, capable of supporting the insurgency."

If we stay, our troops continue to be target practice for these groups, while allowing the insurgency to practice, refine, and sharpen their tactics against us (which can be transplanted to other theaters). The present

Iraqi government doesn't have the ability to govern in our absence, especially since they didn't fight to overthrow Saddam themselves and no natural leaders of the people emerged from that conflict. Without ongoing (perhaps permanent) involvement by the United States, the Iraqi security forces would quickly dissolve.

Against this, the consequences of withdrawal are catastrophic: Iraq descends into civil war. It becomes a Stone Age country with a lot of oil. Al-Qaeda or some similar group gains access to Iraq's oil fields for nearly limitless funding of their operations; the terrorist organization gains another public relations success and recruitment bonanza as our troops leave. The Iraqis who sided with us during the war and occupation are betrayed and left to some hideous fate in the ensuing carnage. So much for Powell's "You broke it, you own it" prewar admonition to President Bush.

But why worry?

As a footnote, we can't help but notice that the Army has exhausted its current supply of fighting forces in Iraq. There are simply no fresh troops to replace the ones that are already overextended there. However, this is easily fixed. All we have to do is use the

National Guard, or break our promise and keep the existing troops there even longer, or break our promise and recall the ones we sent home even sooner. It's just their tough luck. Why should the rest of us be inconvenienced by having to support a larger army when we haven't worn out the one we've got? We could tax ourselves a bit more to build a big enough army. But why? Aren't we still in the Age of Aquarius?

Afghanistan

After our initial post-9/11 success in routing the Taliban in Afghanistan, a Taliban-led insurgency remains a constant threat to the Afghan government, and most of the country is in chaos. The United Nations has ranked Afghanistan on its "top ten" failed-state list. Descriptions from the scene tell how the roads in the countryside are roamed by bands of marauders, with the telephone poles stripped of their wire because copper is more valuable than a telephone system. The country has stepped back centuries.

Its leading export is narcotics (Afghanistan is still the world's leading producer of opium, which becomes heroin), the profitable sale of which is used to fund terrorism. How ironic that American addicts are providing the financial support for the people who are blowing up our soldiers in Iraq. Many top drug lords are leaders in the new government as well, and the civilian population has been completely demoralized by years of conflict. Al-Qaeda is determined to make the country a vanguard Islamic caliphate. Still, why be concerned?

Pakistan

Paradoxically, Pakistan has proven to be a major ally in our war on terrorism, while at the same time being the probable home of some of the top leaders of al-Qaeda. Someday we may go after them in earnest. However, President Musharraf's political fortunes currently hang by a thread, and no one knows how things will shake out. Taliban jihadists are active in his country. Al-Qaeda leadership in Pakistan directed a plan (intercepted, thank God) to bomb in midair nearly a dozen U.S. airliners bound for America in August 2006 using liquid explosives mixed right on board the aircraft.

Pakistan is building stockpiles of nuclear weapons and is working on advanced system designs to increase the effectiveness of the delivery of these weapons.

Maybe everything will work out all right. We can all hope for the best. Peace out, brother.

North Korea

Remember President Ronald Reagan's ridiculous idea of a Strategic Defense Initiative that would build a "missile shield" to protect American cities from nuclear attack? "Star Wars" it was called—remember, ha ha? Now that the insane Kim Jong Il has a store of plutonium from his Yongbyon facility, has tested its first atomic bomb, and has a Taepodong 2 intercontinental ballistic missile (ICBM) capable of delivering a nuclear payload to the United States, some may feel pangs of a nostalgic yearning to return to a time when the government considered protecting its citizens "job one." But no matter. Even if the perpetually cash-strapped Kim only sells the technology in exchange for petrodollars from states like Iran (he has already sold them the missiles), it will still be several years before they're capable of hitting Chicago. There's little to worry about for right now.

In addition to weapons of mass destruction, the Department of Defense believes that North Korea has had a chemical and biological "weapons stockpile of nerve, blister, blood, and choking agents." At a more modest level, North Korea is also developing new intermediate- and short-range ballistic missiles that threaten South Korea, Japan, and the U.S. military in the region. These have already been sold to Iran and several other Middle Eastern countries.

Lebanon

The terrorist group Hezbollah dominates Lebanon's politics, and has the full backing of Iran and Syria (who's believed to have assassinated former Lebanese Prime Minister Rafiq al-Hariri a few years back). After the recent conflict with the Israel Defense Forces, Hezbollah's leadership remains unscathed and its supply of weapons undoubtedly has been replenished from Iran and Syria. It's already the first terrorist group to launch its very own cruise missile. The war with Israel could flare up literally at any time. But this is no business of ours. We can always abandon Israel if necessary—we've abandoned Jews before.

Syria

Syria serves as the major conduit for terrorists (especially the suicide bombers who do most of the headline-making damage) to enter Iraq. The best that can be said is that Syria isn't run by Islamic extremists— no fools, the Syrians.

According to our Department of Defense, Syria has a long-standing chemical-weapons program and a large stockpile of the nerve agent sarin, which can be delivered by aircraft or rockets. Threatened by Israel's superior forces, Syria has pursued a deterrent based on ballistic-missile, chemical, and biological warfare programs. We infer from Israel's recent air strike against an incipient nuclear facility (which Syria acquired from North Korea) that Syria wants to acquire an atomic bomb. More likely, the knowledge-hungry Syrians were only building a research facility, and the Israelis overreacted.

Iran

Iran continues to funnel insurgents into the Iraqi conflict, as well as providing ever-more-sophisticated weaponry for their terrorist attacks. One recent example: bombs that generate molten copper pellets that slice through U.S. Humvee armor. Iran's Revolutionary Guards are a full-fledged terrorist organization, and the nation directly supports terrorism in Afghanistan. No one doubts that President Ahmadinejad would be delighted if a nuclear bomb were to destroy Washington, D.C., or that he'd cheerfully cooperate behind the scenes to make that happen as long as he didn't have to be personally vaporized in response.

In addition to its highly publicized pursuit of the atomic bomb (which may or may not have been temporarily suspended), Iran is believed to be developing its own chemical and biological weapons. It's also developing ballistic missiles capable of hitting Israel and Europe, as well as cruise missiles. It's even working on an antimissile system. Iran has also purchased elaborate defenses, including Russian SA-15 antiaircraft missiles and antiship cruise missiles for deployment in the Persian Gulf. At a minimum, it seeks the ability to disrupt Gulf shipping in the Strait of Hormuz, upon which 30 percent of the world's oil supply depends.

China

The People's Republic of China is in the middle of a tremendous military expansion "focused on improving the quality of military personnel and developing or acquiring long-range, precision-strike missiles, modern fighter aircraft, a blue-water navy, and improved amphibious forces," according to the Defense Intelligence Agency. In short, China seeks to become a global military power on par with its emergence as a global economic power, all under Communist control. As Thomas Donnelly wrote in *The Military We Need:*

> In its burgeoning trade with Iran and oil investments in Sudan, China's engagement with the greater Middle East raises the specter of a genuine "axis of evil"—that is, the kind of direct or indirect strategic cooperation among our enemies. . . . Beijing's indication that it will shield Tehran at the UN Security Council from sanctions over its nuclear program, much as it has protected Khartoum from effective action against the genocide in Darfur, may foreshadow the kind of challenge that lies ahead.

China is already a major supplier of weaponry to sub-Saharan Africa. In 2007, China successfully tested an antisatellite laser on an old weather satellite, raising serious concerns about the vulnerability of our own space-based military assets, upon which so much depends.

China is developing three long-range missile systems—the DF-31 and DF-31A road-mobile ICBMs and the JL-2 submarine-launched ballistic missile (SLBM). Dozens of Chinese ICBMs now target U.S. cities, with many more on the way. China remains committed to developing conventional ballistic missiles capable of reaching U.S. and allied military assets in the region in order to deter intervention if and when they eventually decide to retake Taiwan. It also has a Tomahawk ground-launched cruise missile capable of executing strikes throughout Asia. "Counter-command, control and sensor systems to include communications satellite jammers and ASAT [anti-satellite] weapons, are among Beijing's highest military priorities," McConnell notes, concluding that "China's nuclear capabilities in terms of range, lethality and survivability will increase rapidly over the next ten years."

Russia

Like China, Russia is also in the middle of a major arms buildup. De facto President Putin, an ex-KGB thug ("ex-" for now), longs to restore Russia to its former greatness as an empire, and a strong military is an essential component of his master plan. This country maintains a full complement of nuclear weapons. Although thousands of warheads have been dismantled, Russia relies on nuclear weapons as its primary means of deterrence and continues to improve its munitions. Even if Putin were as benign as Santa Claus, there remains the possibility of an inside terrorist breach of the former Soviet Union's nuclear stockpile.

Having ridden the commodities bull market over the past decade and nationalized its largest oil producer, Russia is flush with cash. Its long-range fighter aircraft are back patrolling the globe and testing our defenses in a way that they haven't since the end of the Cold War. It's making a play in the power vacuum created by so many of our defenses being tied down in Iraq and Afghanistan.

Venezuela

President Hugo Chávez has signed on to Cuba's agenda to remove U.S. influence throughout South America. In a country awash in expensive oil, his policies are destroying the economy in the name of promoting his version of 21st-century socialism. Meanwhile, his government is purchasing weapons from Russia, Iran, and China. Since 2005, Venezuela signed contracts with Russia for 24 Su-30MK2 advanced fighter aircraft; 50 transport and attack helicopters; and 100,000 assault rifles. Chávez has also recently returned from a shopping trip to Russia (spending over $3 billion on arms there in the past two years alone) to purchase submarines and sophisticated antiaircraft defenses, no doubt in anticipation of a future U.S. invasion. Chavez and Iran's President Ahmadinejad have visited each other seven times since 2005.

(*Note:* We just read that Chávez has decided to move the country's clocks ahead a half hour in 2008. He put his science advisor on television to announce the health benefits of the move. This was anticipated years ago by Woody Allen's *Bananas,* wherein a South American dictator announces that henceforth, the official language of San Marcos will be Swedish. "The power has driven him mad," someone whispers.)

Al-Qaeda

As the director of National Intelligence testified before Congress on February 7, 2008: "Al Qaeda is improving the last key aspect of its ability to attack the U.S.: the identification, training and positioning of operatives for an attack in the homeland . . . to focus on prominent political, economic and infrastructure targets designed to produce mass casualties, visually dramatic destruction, significant economic aftershocks, and/or fear among the population."

The doctrines of radical Islam potentially fill a deep-seated psychological void in any Muslim anywhere in the world and can inspire fanatical commitment. Soon these well-funded groups may have access to weapons of mass destruction. Although the United States routinely eliminates al-Qaeda leaders, second-tier members immediately step into leadership roles for their chance in the sun. While we're fortunate that a "second 9/11" hasn't happened on American soil, no one thinks for a moment that such an event can't occur again.

Al-Qaeda is decentralized, and although Osama bin Laden may be out of action, his sidekick Ayman al-Zawahiri is forever imploring Muslims everywhere to take up arms against "the great Satan." Even if they don't succeed in detonating a nuclear warhead in some major Western city or cities, they might succeed in using chemical, biological, or radiological weapons on a smaller scale that would rivet the nation in a new round of terror. In the past, al-Qaeda has shown interest in using ricin, botulinum, cyanide, anthrax, and sarin; and information on how to employ these is widely available on the Internet.

They seem to have no shortage of futureless young people wanting to die for Allah. As we saw in the botched London car explosion attempted by physicians from the UK's National Health Service, cells don't have to get their marching orders from a cave in Pakistan— groups of like-minded murderers can find plenty of avenues to get together on their own.

What Happened?

In 1956, during the heart of the Cold War, defense comprised 60 percent of our country's federal budget; at the same time, welfare programs comprised 22 percent. Today the tables have turned: Even with the wars in Iraq and Afghanistan in process, income redistribution programs compose 60 percent of the budget, while defense is 20 percent. This is as low a level (as a proportion of GDP) of defense funding as has existed during any set of years since World War II. This is a problem. The Office of Management and Budget projects that defense spending will decline even further going forward, to 16 percent of the budget by 2011 (from about 4.1 percent of GDP today to 3.1 percent).

After winning the Cold War without firing a shot, largely through the defense buildup during the Reagan era, our politicians saw fit to eviscerate our defense budget. With no major threat on the horizon (at least, as far as they could see), these spending cuts looked like found money. Since a land war against the Soviets was no longer contemplated, why have a big army? The thinking was that we could maintain a token presence around the world that would buy us enough time to raise troop levels in the unlikely event that they were ever needed. Plus, our allies could be counted upon to stand shoulder to shoulder with us, so only a modest U.S. presence would ever be required.

From 1989 to 1999, the U.S. military was reduced from 2.1 million to 1.4 million men and women. The Army was cut from 18 divisions to 10. President Clinton hacked $196 billion from the defense budget during his two terms in office. Yet at the same time, Presidents George H. W. Bush, Clinton, and George W. Bush have found it necessary to deploy U.S. troops in seven theaters: Panama, the first Gulf War, the Balkans, Haiti, Somalia, Afghanistan, and Iraq.

President George W. Bush rode into Washington with a promise to repair the damage done to our nation's defense by his predecessor—but he wasn't going to just throw money at the problem the way Reagan did in his first term. He was going to use his MBA-oriented approach to fix things intelligently.

With Donald Rumsfeld as his secretary of defense, Bush found a man who could fulfill this mission. Rumsfeld believed that in the future, a few nimble-footed soldiers who were wizards at operating all the latest video-game-like technology would zap our enemies, preferably from the air. The business-school reasoning was this: Let's play up the competitive advantage that gives us our edge.

When the war in Iraq loomed, the shortcomings of this approach became apparent. We raced to Baghdad, captured the flag, and then the country went to hell around us, both for a lack of planning and for a lack of what later came to be called "boots on the ground." This shouldn't have been a great surprise: of these eight major military operations we spoke of since 1989, five have required long-term deployment of significant American forces. So did the rebuilding of Germany after World War II and South Korea after the Korean War— we're still in both places in significant numbers. We did exit Vietnam precipitously, but that led to catastrophe for those we left behind. Meanwhile, despite all the money spent on the war effort, the net effect has been to further postpone the necessary expenditures on new systems acquisition.

Bush did raise military pay and benefits—which was long overdue—but this had the effect of making sol-diers seem like an expensive commodity that could be cut back once smaller numbers of them were equipped with the latest gizmos. Now service members are better paid, but they must pay a price in another way, being rotated more frequently on longer deployments away from their families.

The United States has had a faux military buildup since 9/11. We're spending more dollars on defense, but we're in a weaker position than we were before.

The wars in Afghanistan and Iraq have been incredibly costly, and they've consumed vast amounts of ordnance. As a mechanic will tell you, grinding tanks, Bradley fighting vehicles, and Humvees through the sand year after year doesn't do them any good. That's why thousands of them sit idle at Army depots, awaiting repair. Meanwhile, merely getting the sand out of their gears does nothing to make up the $50 billion equipment shortfall we faced at the time the conflict began. Our valiant troops are tired, and we don't have the reserves we need. If another war were to come upon us, we'd be in no position to fight it.

This is where our armed forces stand after the sixth year of our "war on terror":

Army

As of August 2007, we had about 150,000 soldiers in the field, and an active duty force of some 500,000. Combat tours lasting six months in the 1990s are now extended to more than a year for most troops in Middle Eastern theaters, with many soldiers now looking at third tours of duty in the region in a conflict that has gone on longer than World War II. By opting for not adding manpower, we have only about 10,000 soldiers not presently deployed who are ready to take on any new military challenge(!). Imagine how this limits the President's options in dealing with international contingencies.

Air Force

According to Air Force chief of staff General T. Michael Moseley, the Air Force is $20 billion short of funds for this year and for each succeeding year.

The F-22 fighter has been slated for early termination, while the F-15s it was designed to replace are suffering from age-related metal fatigue. Most of our long-range bombers were made when John F. Kennedy was President, but even these are newer than our reconnaissance planes, which were developed under President Eisenhower. The average plane in the Air Force is now older than the average warship in the Navy. While our planes get older, our enemies are installing new air-defense systems that can stop all but the most advanced stealth bombers. Heaven help the pilots who might someday be sent against these systems. Remember that the mighty country of Serbia has already shot down one of our stealth fighters.

Navy

The 600-ship Navy of the 1980s is now a 279-ship Navy. We hope that these ships are all well equipped to fend off the cruise missiles our enemies are stockpiling everywhere, but we wouldn't be surprised to learn otherwise. Fortunately, everyone else's navies are so far behind ours that we still have a numeric advantage. Whether it will be a sufficient presence to keep China from invading Taiwan remains to be seen.

Marine Corps

The 2006 Quadrennial Defense Review proposed downsizing our Marine Corps by 5,000 men and women. Yet according to Frank Hoffman of the U.S. Marine Corps Center for Emerging Threats and Opportunities, we need more Marines, not fewer, if we're going the give the President the option of using these troops for the tasks for which they have traditionally been sent: amphibious landings and kicking the doors down in hostile cities to throw the bad guys out. This is going to require about 20,000 more Marines than we have at present.

Where Do We Go?

According to military analyst Frederick Kagan, this leads to an unavoidable conclusion: "Unless we move to increase the size of the Army and the Marines, the U.S. military will be far weaker when President Bush leaves office than it was when he took power—despite having acquired a mammoth new mission called the war on terror."

There are enormous challenges facing the United States in the decades ahead. We're presently fighting wars in Iraq and Afghanistan, where there will be drastic consequences from our failure to win. We are fighting a global war on terror that has brought the battleground onto U.S. soil to U.S. civilians. The first priority of government is to protect its citizens. If our government can't do that, then not much else that it might do really matters. It is time to restore Franklin Roosevelt's freedom from fear.

The world will continue to be the dangerous place it has always been. Who can say what threats might emerge from Iran or from China, Russia, Pakistan, or Islamofascism? What about the threats we don't list here because we don't foresee them, which are usually the worst kind? The United States military will stand up to these threats. Our country needs to make sure its military is more than adequate to meet the tasks it is sent to do.

Our army presently consists of about 500,000 troops. These should be restored to the 750,000 troops that the United States had during the 1970s and 1980s. We need to aggressively pursue all the deferred upgrading of our weapons systems that have been mercilessly struck from budget after budget. In short, we need another Ronald Reagan to come to Washington, someone who is determined to make America strong again. This renewed commitment will help us win in the Middle East, defeat Islamic fundamentalism, and put our enemies on notice that they'd better think long and hard before mounting foreign ventures against our interests.

The U.S. is a rich country and can afford what it needs to invest in its own defense. Dedicating 5 percent of this country's GDP—one nickel on the dollar—to securing our national defense would be a good place to start. If we follow the present course instead, our ability to fight will diminish. The gap between what our military is called upon to do and what it will be able to deliver will widen. The world will grow even more dangerous for Americans.

Gratitude for Our Armed Forces

We read constantly of hedge-fund managers earning hundreds of millions of dollars a year. We read of the lavish parties given by CEOs who loot the companies entrusted to them by shareholders. Our country is at war, yet life goes on as usual in the cities, with fine dining, drinking, getting, and spending, as if it were the *fin de siècle.* We put movie stars on the covers of our magazines. Meanwhile, the officers and enlisted service members who barely scrape by on military pay, but who guard the nation in Afghanistan and Iraq, on ships and in submarines and near the Arctic Circle, are anonymous as they live and as they die.

Who makes all of this ordinary life possible? The guy who faces desert heat every day wearing full body armor with no air-conditioning and brutal killers laying explosives for him and sniping at him—and her—at every turn.

God bless this glorious American military—every wife, every child, and every parent—and endless prayers for them to return home safe, mission accomplished. God bless them every moment of every day for keeping safe this America, inside of which we live as powerfully as we inhabit our own skin. This has to be the central fact of our lives: gratitude for the men and women who make our lives possible, who wear the uniform and cover it with glory.

How can we ever thank them and their families? How can we possibly repay the sacrifice that they make? How can it ever be enough?

What about the Army and Marine Corps wives who go to sleep in their king-size beds alone for a year? What about the Army Ranger's wife who just heard that her husband won't be coming home from Afghanistan? What about the child whose father will never teach him how to hit a ball or parallel park because he's in a military cemetery?

It is true that they have something the rest of us rarely possess: meaning. They know why God put them on Earth, why they live and suffer. They never doubt their worth.

Our lives are measured by what we do for others, not by how much money we make. Spending time with lonely people, military families, widows, and widowers is a pretty easy way to make a huge difference in a suffering human life. So when you think of your uncle who just lost his wife, when you think of the woman down the street whose husband was just called up by the National Guard and sent to Iraq, don't just think about them. Ask them out to dinner, invite them to a barbecue, or just call them up to gossip.

Certainly military pay should be increased—through raising taxes on the rest of us if necessary—which it will be. We need a commitment to treat the families of the military like gold. We also recommend supporting organizations like Tragedy Assistance Program for Survivors, which provides social and emotional support to the surviving families of those who have died in service to America. Another organization called Soldiers' Angels sends care packages, letters, and other aid to military personnel and their families. If you give them $100, it means a lot. There is also the Folded Flag Foundation, which takes in donations and gives the money to the families of service members killed fighting for us. There are many other such organizations. You will find ways to help if you look.

✷　✷　✷

Chapter
Five

Be a Country
Without Borders

☆ ☆

The philosopher Ludwig Wittgenstein invited his students to perform the following thought experiment. See if it works for you.

- Imagine a song you know well.

- Then imagine the song, but without the lyrics.

Got it?

Okay, proceed to part two.

- Now imagine the song without the lyrics and without the music.

Unless you are some kind of mystic, what you are probably left imagining is . . . nothing. Certainly, it's nothing that resembles the song you originally had in mind.

Taking a page from Ludwig's playbook, let's modify the experiment:

- Imagine the United States of America.

- Now, imagine the United States of America without any borders.

Our guess is that whatever you're left thinking about—if anything—probably doesn't bear much resemblance to the country we know and love.

This experiment is presently being carried out in the real world, under our noses, right on our watch, engineered by our elected representatives, even though it's opposed by the general population. What gives?

Who's Responsible for the Immigration Problem

For most of our nation's history, immigration was not a major social issue. The population proliferated mostly by natural means until the 1850s, when waves of immigrants from northern and western Europe began to arrive. These newcomers fit in pretty well with the dominant WASP culture. By the turn of the century, however, those who were seen as less-desirable types from eastern and southern Europe began arriving in significant numbers. The involvement of immigrant anarchists in the Haymarket Riot in Chicago in 1886 did nothing to improve their reputation. With the Immigration Act of 1924, a quota system was finally put in place, allowing in only so many immigrants of each nationality every year. This system held for the next 40 years. During this time, there was no net immigration at all.

What happened to change all this? Astonishingly, the blame can largely be laid at the door of . . . Ted Kennedy! Passed as part of the gaseous "Great Society" agenda, the Immigration and Nationality Act Amendments of 1965 were pushed through the Senate by the bloviator himself. At one stroke, the bill abolished the national quota system which had served our country so well for half a century. It stemmed the tide from Europe and promoted immigration from the third world.

Kennedy told Americans not to worry about opening the floodgates—the gesture was just "symbolic." It turned out to be symbolic to the tune of more than 28 million new immigrants (all potential constituents of the Democrats' social services handouts, and hence new recruits to the party once they were made voters). And those were only the legal ones. While the bill was supposed to open immigration to a wider variety of nationalities, it had exactly the opposite effect: Our immigrants now come primarily from Mexico and Latin America. Our country's immigration policy drove right off a bridge.

The loss of border control was entirely one way. Peter Brimelow, author of *Alien Nation*, recounts his inquiry as to what it would take to turn the tables and immigrate from the U.S. to Mexico. Calling the Mexican Embassy, he was told:

> Unless you are hired by a Mexican company that obtains a temporary work permit, or are a retiree older than sixty-five who can prove financial self-sufficiency, you must get a six-month tourist visa, and apply in person to the Ministry of the Interior

in Mexico City. If your visa expires before the process is complete, you must get a new visa and begin again.

This from a country that sends 200,000 to 300,000 legal and illegal immigrants to the U.S. every year, Brimelow observes. (Brimelow's Website **www.vdare. com** is an excellent source of information on the immigration debate.)

To cope with the problems created by the 1965 legislation, Congress passed the Immigration Reform and Control Act in 1986. The 1986 act was supposed to offer amnesty to a million undocumented workers, but in all, three million immigrants were legalized. The act also created penalties for employers who hired illegal immigrants. However, enforcement hasn't been pervasive. In 2004, exactly three employers were fined for hiring illegal aliens. Meanwhile, more than a half-million U.S. workers report having the following social security number: 000-00-0000. We suspect that at least 499,999 of these are bogus, and frankly, we're not too sure about that last guy, either.

Then the Immigration Act of 1990 put a ceiling of 700,000 legal immigrants a year, a limit that has been widely ignored. In 2006, legal permanent-resident status was granted to 1,266,264 people. How did this happen?

Who's Here

There are about 26 million legal immigrants in the United States, or about 9 percent of the total population. There are many roads leading to Rome.

The most obvious end run around the 1990 ceiling is the fact that an unlimited number of family members (spouses, parents, and children) of U.S. citizens are automatically exempted. To a lesser extent, adult children, siblings, and their spouses and children are also welcomed. All total, we allowed in 580,483 people this way in 2006, and this method generally accounts for about half of all legal immigration.

Thus, an illegal-immigrant woman in labor who presents herself at an emergency room in San Diego can't be turned away, and her baby is a U.S. citizen and a ticket into this country's vast supermarket of social services for her entire family. For an even bigger payday, she can sue the doctors and the hospital if she didn't like the outcome of her treatment. Some

383,000 "anchor babies" are born in our country every year, one in ten of all U.S. births.

Another common tactic is for an illegal alien to get his or her ticket punched by marrying a U.S. citizen, giving rise to the marriage of convenience and the sham marriage broker. This puts our immigration service in the position of judge and jury as to whether each marriage presented to them is legit or not.

In addition to admitting family members of its citizens, the United States also admits foreigners for humanitarian reasons. These include refugees who ostensibly can't return to their native countries for fear of persecution due to race, religion, politics, and the like. We also let people remain here who are seeking asylum—essentially, refugees who are already inside our borders. Once this status is granted, they immediately receive a "green card," entitling them to permanent residence in the U.S., and are presented with a menu of social services. Peter Brimelow has observed that over 80 percent of refugees and asylees have relatives already living in the United States, which suggests that they may not constitute a truly random sampling from globally persecuted peoples. Very possibly, the system is being gamed. In 2006, the U.S. admitted 216,454 refugees and asylees.

A third broad category of foreigners in our midst are various kind of guest workers. These "temporary" additions to the labor force come into the U.S. to work for specific employers. American agriculture imports unskilled labor through the H-2A program, while skilled workers are invited in via H-1B visas.

These H-1B workers can stay legally for up to six years, and this often leads to a green card as well. Although their numbers are technically capped at 65,000, some 407,818 entered the country in 2006 because universities and nonprofit organizations can apply for an unlimited number.

H-2B workers are another group, which include students, construction workers, and seasonal work-ers in tourist areas (hotel maids, for example). They're allowed to bring in their spouses and children, and of course once a baby is born here, the family would be exceedingly difficult to deport even if our government cared enough to bother, which it doesn't.

Are you concerned that there isn't enough diver-sity in America today? Worry not. The United States also runs a "diversity lottery" that allows immigrants in at random. Every year, 50,000 winning numbers are picked from applications sent in from all over the world. The only entry requirement is a desire to come to the United States, for whatever reason. Some element of fraud is found in most applications, as people submit multiple entries under different names. Strange to say, the winners are disproportionately from Muslim countries.

Finally, there are millions of foreigners who come into our nation every year on temporary visas as tourists, students, or on business. While they're only supposed to stay for 90 days, they can fail to leave after their visas expire, and no one goes looking for them.

No one knows how many illegal immigrants are in the United States. The government has an incentive to undercount and dismiss the problem, while illegals themselves have no incentive to self-identify to the census officials with clipboards who come around to count them. The government estimates that there might be between 8 and 12 million in all, while unofficial estimates put this number considerably higher—even twice as high. Whatever the exact figure is, everyone agrees that it's increasing, perhaps by another 500,000 a year, to use one widely cited figure.

Most illegal immigrants are Mexicans who have come here looking for higher-paying jobs than they can find south of the (former) border. The U.S. Citizenship and Immigration Services estimate that in addition to these, there are approximately 78,000 illegal aliens from countries who are of special concern in the war on terror.

In all, the foreign-born population of our country might be 10 to 15 percent of the total U.S. population, depending on whose numbers we believe.

We're told that the United States is a nation of immigrants. Presumably, this would be true of every country in the world except Ethiopia, where the first human beings are supposed to have swung down from trees a couple of hundred thousand years ago. The human race has been collecting frequent-flier miles ever since, such that by now pretty much everyone is from somewhere else. Additionally, some people—through no merit of their own—have advantages and disadvantages that other people don't. Some children are born in Beverly Hills, while others are born in Darfur. We're not sure what the implications of these truisms are for our nation's immigration policy, but we wanted to acknowledge them before proceeding further.

Costs and Benefits

To economists, the idea of open borders—like open markets—has a lot of appeal. It's axiomatic that the market will sort out the allotment of labor and capital to the highest and best use far better than a group of government planners will. So let us concede that in an ideal world, there might be no borders at all, just like on R. Buckminster Fuller's Dymaxion Map.

That said, this economic benefit isn't the supernal good that transcends all other goods. It has to be weighed against other considerations, such as national security, to name one. The costs and the benefits of the current arrangement fall on different shoulders. Let's tease these apart.

Based on the work of economist Donald Huddle (*The Net National Costs of Immigration: Fiscal Effects of Welfare Restorations to Legal Immigrants*), the total net fiscal cost of immigration could be reasonably estimated between $80 and $110 billion annually. This is primarily because immigrants typically have less than a high school education. Because they have low skills, they earn low wages; and under our progressive tax system, they pay little in the way of taxes. At the same time, their relative poverty entitles them to U.S. welfare services, including Medicaid, free medical treatment, food stamps, and free public school (complete with free lunches) for their children. According to the Center for Immigration Studies, 24 percent are on Medicaid, 29 percent receive welfare, and 30 percent are eligible for the earned income tax credit. Immigrants constitute 19 percent of all children in our public schools, not to mention their use of the legal systems and prisons, all provided at taxpayer expense.

An immigrant with less than a high school degree will use $89,000 more in taxes and services in the course of his lifetime than he pays in taxes. Only Social Security and Medicare are utilized proportionately more by natives than by immigrants, but that is only due to immigrants' younger age. As economist and Nobel laureate Milton Friedman pointed out, open borders are incompatible with the welfare state.

Who benefits? First of all, the immigrants themselves, who earn far more here than they could back home. So do their political leaders, who have a vested interest in the proliferation of their supporters, as well as the people who arrange the immigrants' entry into the United States. Government bureaucracies benefit from having as large a constituency as possible, even at a net cost to taxpayers. Then there are the employers— the people who run the farms, factories, construction projects, restaurants, and hotels where the low cost of labor makes their enterprises cheaper to run than they otherwise would be. Some of this imported deflation is passed on to consumers and investors.

Eventually, as the children, grandchildren, and great-grandchildren of today's immigrants become better educated, their progeny should make a net positive fiscal contribution, generations hence. Just as our better-educated immigrants do today.

While the benefits of our current immigration arrangements are relatively targeted, the costs are more diffuse. They're mostly borne by that hapless fellow behind the tree, the U.S. taxpayer, who's footing the bill for the social-infrastructure build-out to accommodate all the newcomers. It's one of those situations where, as the famous economist and father of one of your authors, Herbert Stein, once said, the constant "ME" is always greater than the variable "U."

The proponents of open immigration are vocal and focused, while the opponents are numerous but disorganized. The costs come down especially hard on people living in areas with high concentrations of unskilled immigrants (New Jersey, California, and the Southwest generally), as various social services are mandated at the federal level but are paid for at the state level. It's estimated that every illegal immigrant in California consumes $8 to $12 of public services for every $1 he or she contributes in taxes, making this subsidy a meaningful percentage of the average Californian's tax return.

Almost as an afterthought, it also hurts native low-skilled U.S. workers, another constituency no one really cares about. It's often said that immigrants only do jobs that native workers don't want, but in economic terms, this is nonsense. As Steven Camarota of the Center for Immigration Studies has pointed out, there's no such thing as a majority immigrant occupation. "Most of the people who clean toilets in America, the vast majority are native born; most of the people who are nannies and busboys, native born." If the illegals coming in all had law degrees and licenses to practice before the bar, our borders would have been sealed long ago.

A National Identity Without Borders

Another cost, unfashionable to mention, is that—unlike in previous waves of immigration in our nation's history—many in the latest wave of immigrants seem to have little interest in assimilating themselves into the mainstream of American life. They want to maintain their separate nationalist identities, languages, and traditions—as it were, to assimilate the United States back into Mexico ("la reconquista"). One-tenth of Mexico's population now lives in the United States—a land that 58 percent of its citizens consider rightfully their own, according to one survey. Never mind that if we hadn't taken over the sparsely settled territory, the economy of the American Southwest would today resemble that of . . . well, Mexico, to the detriment of the entire world. There would be no reason for anyone to come to San Diego if the city were just "North Tijuana."

More broadly, over one-third of all people ever to reach America have arrived here subsequent to 1970. We wonder, for example, whether these new arrivals feel the patriotic swelling of pride in America and its history and institutions that characterized the immigrants of previous generations, or a willingness to take up arms to defend our way of life. If not, this poses its own risk to our national identity, unless our national identity is to be a culture without borders.

As Peter Brimelow starkly portrays it, "There are going to be a small number of very wealthy people living in gated communities and a very large number of very poor people sort of scuffling around out there in the dirt. And the one is going to have to be protected from the other." In other words, America is going to become Brazil. As parts of America are transformed into a third-world country, we're comforted with the admonition that we should "celebrate diversity." "Diversity," here as elsewhere, means "shut up if you disagree."

The Social-Engineering Experiment

Our country's population is now about 303 million people. With greater affluence, family size drops to replacement levels, meaning that the population stabilizes (and would have stabilized years ago at a lower level). However, because the government has effectively superimposed an open-borders policy, our population is instead growing rapidly. The U.S. Census Bureau estimates that by the year 2050, the population will clock in at *420 million people.* Of those, 140 million will be post-1970 immigrants and their offspring.

If they continue to settle in the Southwest, a desert, we wonder where the fresh drinking water is going to come from, to cite but one troubling question.

Many of the costs imposed by immigration policy are what economists call "negative externalities" that are difficult to measure. Writer/director Ronald F. Maxwell (*Gettysburg, Gods and Generals*) pointedly describes some of these:

> Where was the concern for American schoolchildren forced to sit in overcrowded classes, for American patients forced to wait in overcrowded hospitals, for American workers whose wages are being undercut, for American drivers forced to sit in interminable traffic jams in over-whelmed freeway systems, for the victims of organized gangs, for the American college students who are turned away from publicly funded state universities, for many African Americans who are being literally displaced from their neighborhoods while being moved figuratively, once again, to the back of the bus, for those environmentalists and conservationists who want to protect open space and slow down urban sprawl, for the American taxpayers who have had to bear the burden of billions of dollars in increased welfare costs, over-burdened prisons, extra police and security and even, adding insult to injury, for bilingual education?

Even if, in the long run, the immigrants are all wonderfully assimilated and make America a paradise in 2050, this will be on the backs of the people who paid for the social experiment today. Take all the commuters going to work in Southern California and imagine that it takes them an extra five or ten minutes to get to work each day because of the supercongested freeways they're forced to share with all the immigrants. Multiply this figure by the value of their time, and this is an astronomical outlay all by itself. The rate at which newcomers are brought in is extremely pertinent to the people who are already here, who have to bear the costs of absorbing them. We get cheaper strawberries and leaf blowing, but at an exorbitant overall cost.

National Security

The staggering failure of our government to fulfill its most elementary duty—the protection of private citizens from foreign aggression—became apparent on 9/11. Some people might think that the lack of a follow-up strike by foreign terrorists here signifies that all is well and the government is now doing a great job. Your authors would respectfully disagree.

The immigration service deals out a million green cards every year granting permanent U.S. residency to foreigners. No one denies that the system is overwhelmed and that screening is inadequate. A sizeable percentage of applications involve outright fraud. In addition, there are 400,000 people whom a judge has ordered to leave for one reason or another, but who are still here because there's no effective follow-up enforcement.

The idea of granting amnesty to illegals is often bruited as a "solution" to the immigration problem, but adding millions of new applications to the pile is going to make the problem worse. One of the people who got amnesty last time was Mahmoud Abu Halima. He then made several trips to Afghanistan to receive terrorist training, and came back and bombed the World Trade Center in 1993. Mohammed Salameh was correctly denied a green card, but since no one actually made him leave, he elected to stay. He rented the Ryder truck used in the 1993 attack.

Here's another bad guy: Ghazi Ibrahim Abu Mezer. He was arrested in New York City in 1997 for planning to bomb its subway system. He'd been caught three times before, each time for illegally entering the country from

Canada. At the time of his last arrest, he was out on bail, facing deportation hearings. Meanwhile, he had—no joke—applied for political asylum. Terrorists play our legal system like a Stradivarius.

The State Department refused only 32 immigrant visas in the year 2000 on security grounds. The 19 terrorists who executed the 9/11 attacks all entered the country legally on six-month visas. Talk about documentation: They held 63 state drivers' licenses among them. After 9/11, the fiscal year 2002 saw only 27, or 0.1 percent, of immigrant visas denied for national security reasons. This makes us wonder if enforcement is as tough as it should be.

Is it really fair to exclude someone from our country merely because he wants to destroy it? Don't Americans believe in freedom of speech and freedom of worship? What about "I do my thing and you do your thing," as embodied in Fritz Perls's Gestalt Prayer?

The answer is that we have a long-standing tradition—going back to before 1776—of turning away people we don't want. Remember that the colonies were used as a dumping ground for convicts and other social undesirables, and the colonists didn't like this. Our first laws included provisions to keep out anyone who couldn't support him- or herself, as well as those who posed moral or security threats. As James R. Edwards, Jr., of the Hudson Institute wrote: "First as colonies, then as states, early Americans sought to preserve and protect the character of the society they and their forefathers paid so high a price to establish." Maybe we ought to do the same.

This tradition continued right up through the Cold War, when people were excluded simply for being Communists—that is, believing in a totalitarian ideology bent on the destruction of the West. With the end of the Cold War, it became unfashionable to exclude foreigners for any such reason. But Islamofascism is the same song, just with new mumbo jumbo for lyrics. There's no reason for us to automatically extend to aliens the rights that we reserve for our own citizens.

Additionally, our Visa Waiver Program needs serious enforcement. This program allows visitors from friendly nations like Great Britain and those in western Europe to come to the United States for three months without any visa at all, just traveling on a passport. The London suicide bombings of July 7, 2005 were run by people who fell exactly into this category. Imagine how simple it would have been for London-subway bomber Germaine Lindsay, a 19-year-old Islamic convert, to visit his mother in Cleveland, Ohio; or for shoe bomber "Richard Colvin Reid," as he was politely referred to by *The New York Times,* but whose real name was Abdul Raheem, to get on a plane to come here. The point is that with 15 to 20 million Muslims now living in Europe, it's no longer safe to presume who our friends are based on their country of citizenship.

The day after Islamic terrorists detonate an atomic bomb in a major U.S. metropolitan area and hundreds of thousands of our countrymen and women lie dead and dying, are we going hit ourselves on the forehead and exclaim, "Gee, we never saw this coming! With our country's incredibly tight border control, it just doesn't seem possible that these bad guys got in." No, we're going to be outraged that politicians fiddled while leaving our country to burn.

Policy Solutions

The sooner we dismiss the idea of mass amnesty, the better. Apart from serving no purpose, what could be more insulting to those naturalized citizens who have played by the rules? We aren't fans of police roundups of illegals in a campaign of mass exportation, either. Winnowing the immigrant population through attrition seems like a reasonable way to proceed.

All employees should have to present valid documents establishing their right to work in the United States, and companies that skirt this requirement should be heavily fined. The IRS should stop accepting bogus Social Security numbers, and illegals shouldn't be able to claim tax refunds or otherwise participate in our economic life by opening bank accounts in the U.S. Only 4 percent of our southern border is fenced—this isn't enough. Our borders need to be guarded. If this is expensive, then so be it.

The U.S. Department of Homeland Security ought to go after those people still living here whose temporary visas have expired and show them the door. Everyone coming into our country on temporary visas ought to be carefully screened. Immigration inspectors at our borders need to be given broad discretion to turn away anyone who appears suspicious. The presumption should be that entering the United States is a privilege, not an automatic right, with the burden of proof on the foreigner to prove that he's a friendly. Intelligence about potential terrorists needs to be shared in databases readily accessible to those guarding our borders.

These are just some ideas. Undoubtedly, there are much better ones out there. The point is that we ought to have wide-open borders for people who love America and who will contribute more to our society than they take. These immigrants raise the standard of living for everyone. We ought to close our borders to people who hate America or who otherwise will be parasites on the American dream.

Chapter
Six

Practice Voodoo
Economics

In 1931, the House of Representatives, in an effort to alleviate the effects of . . . Anyone? Anyone? The Great Depression passed the . . . Anyone? The Smoot-Hawley Tariff Act which—anyone? —raised or lowered? (Pause) Raised tariffs in an effort to collect more revenue. Did it work? Anyone know the effects? Anyone? (Pause) It did not work and the United States sank deeper into the Great Depression. Today, we have a similar debate over this: (A screech of chalk as the teacher draws a curve on blackboard) Anyone know what this is? Anyone seen this before? The Laffer curve.

*Anyone? Anyone? Anyone know what this says?
(Pause) It says that at this point on the revenue
curve (He points) you will get exactly the same
amount of revenue as at this point. (He points)
Does anyone know what Mr. Bush called this?
Anyone? Something-doo economics? Voodoo economics.*

— Ben Stein in
Ferris Bueller's Day Off

A time-tested way to ruin a nation is for its leaders to engage in economic malpractice. During the
1930s, our government took a stock-market crash and
amplified it (via a tight money policy from the Federal
Reserve Board) into the Great Depression, whereby it
nearly sank the country altogether.

Today, our government is engaged in economic
malpractice of a different sort:

- Running large deficits during times of
  prosperity, despite the fact that we face
  potential financial liabilities of catastrophic
  proportions going forward

- Pushing the Kool-Aid of supply-side economics that says cutting taxes gives us money for nothing

- Persecuting the oil industry—an industry vital to our survival

The Deficit and the National Debt

We're running a federal budget deficit of roughly $163 billion for fiscal 2007 (not counting off-budget items such as Social Security and Medicare). This annual deficit is slated to grow to $244 billion for 2008.

The standard Republican refrain is that we should pare spending to the bone. How lovely this would be. However, the sad fact is that spending rises every year, no matter what people want or say they want. Every President and every member of Congress promises to cut "needless" and "wasteful" spending, but spending has risen every year since 1940 except for a few years after World War II and a brief period following the Korean War.

It would be great to disband the Department of Education and send the bureaucrats packing, to pick one federal program out of many that could be eliminated with immediate social benefits. We have a Republican President, a Republican Congress, and what do we get instead? "No Child Left Behind." The budget for the Department of Education grew from $42.2 billion in 2001 to $56 billion today. What's sadder still is that even if we did do the right thing and eliminate the Department of Education altogether, it's still peanuts in the context of the overall $2.9 trillion federal budget.

Today the imperatives for spending are built into the system, and with entitlements expanding rapidly, increased spending is locked in. Medicare, Social Security, interest on the national debt—all of these are growing like mad, and no one knows how they'll ever be stopped or even slowed appreciably. We are on a runaway train.

When you spend more money than you take in every year, you go into debt. That's exactly what our country has done—our current national indebtedness amounts to $9.1 trillion. We have deficits such as have never been dreamed of in the absence of a world war, with more than $2 trillion added to the total national debt since 2001 alone. Just the service on this debt cost the country (and by the country, we mean you and me) $406 billion in 2006. This is the third-biggest line item in the entire budget—surpassed only by our income redistribution programs (to a politician, this is money for votes) and national defense.

Meanwhile, the discounted present value of the total future unfunded liabilities from Social Security and Medicare (that is, what we're projected to take in versus what we're on the hook to pay out) is estimated at $88.2 trillion as of 2007. This is a staggering amount, equal to roughly six times our country's gross domestic product. If you spread the liability among every citizen living today, it would amount to a debt of $290,000 per man, woman, and child. While most of the lip service is paid to the impending bankruptcy of Social Security, that's really the smallest of our worries here. The unfunded liability for the new drug benefit that Congress put on our credit cards in 2006 is greater than the entire Social Security deficit all by itself.

The truth is that we have no plans to pay this debt ourselves. We're going to kick the can down the road and make it someone else's problem—namely, that of our children and grandchildren. The longer we string along without addressing the issue, the more drastic the eventual solution will have to be. At present, Social Security and Medicare burn through 4 percent of our nation's general revenues. In the year 2030, they're slated to engulf 34.2 percent.

The economy isn't going to just "grow" the problem away, unless you think that old age, medical, and health-care costs are going to shrink as the baby boomers retire while the rest of the economy expands. The projections run in precisely the opposite direction. Nationalizing health care ("Hillarycare") won't make it cheaper, either—just more unpleasant, as a visit to the doctor becomes more like a visit to the Department of Motor Vehicles. As Nobel laureate and economist Milton Friedman wrote in a Hoover Institution report:

> The effect of tax exemption and the enactment of Medicare and Medicaid on rising medical costs from 1946 to now is clear. According to my estimates, the two together accounted for nearly 60 percent of the total increase in cost. . . . Government's share went from an eighth of the total in 1919 to a quarter in 1965 to nearly half in 1997.

Government-sponsored health care will only be cheaper if we consume less of it, via the mechanism of administrative rationing by pitiless bureaucrats.

There are those who say that "deficits don't matter." This would be nice if it were true. We pay $5 billion a week of interest on the deficit, a lot of it to overseas owners of our debt, such as our good friends in OPEC, negatively impacting the value of the dollar. It matters at a number of levels. For one thing, we have to work a large part of the year just to pay the interest. Congress has made all of us debtors on an endlessly growing installment-plan debt.

If deficits don't really matter, why bother to even discuss balancing the budget? Why have taxes at all? Why not just print money the way Weimar Germany did? Why don't we all just drop acid, turn on, tune in, and drop out of responsibility in the fiscal area? Why not spend as much as we want on anything we want?

Take a Walk on the Supply Side

Traditionally, conservatives were in favor of a balanced budget. The conservative position was that it's not okay to leave heavy burdens of indebtedness to our grandchildren. The conservative view was that there should be some balance between income and outflow. When did this change?

It changed when the idea began to gain currency that we could cut taxes and thereby generate so much revenue that this would automatically balance the budget all by itself. This sounds appealing in the context of a political campaign, when candidates who should know better push each other out of the way to claim that raising taxes (bad) actually lowers total revenue, while cutting taxes (good) stimulates federal revenue. This is called "supply side" economics, since the tax cuts are supposed to create incentives for people to supply more goods and services. The term "supply side" was coined by economist Herbert Stein (your author Ben Stein's father) in 1976.

Supply side wears a halo of respectability borrowed from economist Milton Friedman. Professor Friedman claimed that cutting taxes would starve the monster of government, preventing the state from being so big and intrusive and such a threat to our civil liberties. That makes sense if you have a government of responsible adults.

Then along came Arthur Laffer, an intelligent and very likable man who, with no substantial data in support of his conclusion, asserted that if you cut taxes on income, you'd stimulate so much economic activity that you'd collect as much in taxes as you did before, when rates were higher.

This was a refinement on Keynesian economics, which predicted that economic growth would follow if you cut taxes and ran a deficit because the government would spend at a higher rate than consumers. John Maynard Keynes didn't have a lot of data for his theories, either, but they appealed to President Franklin D. Roosevelt, so they were tried on a tiny scale during the Depression. They didn't work then, however, because the scale of the deficits was far too small. But they worked like gangbusters in World War II, when federal deficits were running at roughly 40 percent of the gross national product and the economy was exploding with growth.

What we saw in the years of President Ronald Reagan—and now under the Presidency of George W. Bush—was not at all a vindication of Professor Friedman or Mr. Laffer.

Cutting taxes hasn't produced the federal-spending cuts that Professor Friedman was hoping for— not even close. Federal spending as a percentage of GDP barely changed under President Reagan. We cut taxes but went on spending like before, only more so. Meanwhile, the gusher of income-tax receipts that was promised to shrink the deficit to as low or lower than the level before the tax cuts didn't materialize. Federal revenues fell dramatically, then rose, but nowhere near enough to make up for the tax losses.

While we have a strong economy by many metrics, this isn't a redemption of supply-side theory, which promised enough growth to cause tax receipts to rise by more than the dollars lost to the tax cuts. In practice, supply-side economics is just vote buying.

Mr. Reagan and the current President Bush were and are the real Keynesian disciples, not FDR or any other Democrat. The Republicans turn out to be the party of Keynes, as President Richard M. Nixon long ago acknowledged when he famously declared in 1971: "Now I am a Keynesian. We are all Keynesians now."

We'd all like to believe that we can get something for nothing. And like you, we hate taxes. Supply side is fun in the same way it's fun to rationalize spending as if it were saving, and in the same way any theory is fun when it says that the easier, softer way is better than the hard way. Wouldn't it be pretty if it were true?

The problem with the "supply-side" prescription becomes apparent if we ask by what mechanism the hay of tax cuts is spun into gold in the federal Treasury. "Supply-side" economists say that by lowering taxes, we create more prosperity and more tax revenue because we stimulate economic activity. With taxes cut, we keep more of what we earn, so we'll work harder— that is, work more hours.

How else could income-tax cuts stimulate economic activity except by encouraging Americans to work more or else by having more people in the labor force? The miller's daughter will be incentivized to spend more time at her spinning wheel.

But the very opposite might be true. It could equally be the case that if we get to keep more of what we earn, we won't need to work as hard, so we'll work less. In fact, the number of hours Americans work per week has barely budged in the five years since President Bush's tax cuts, and it's very much less than the number of hours worked per week on average in 1959, when the top tax bracket was nearly 80 percent. Moreover, overall labor-force participation has almost not moved at all since the Bush tax cuts were passed.

If the personal income-tax cuts aren't working to stimulate the economy through added labor, then just how *are* they working. Through wires too thin to see? Or are they, in fact, working?

The federal government collected roughly $1 trillion in income taxes from individuals in fiscal year 2000, the last full year of President Bill Clinton's merry rule. It fell to a low of $794 billion in 2003 after Mr. Bush's tax cuts and the effects of the recession. Only by the end of fiscal year 2006 did income-tax revenue surpass the $1 trillion level again. To be fair, tax receipts on corporate profits increased, as those profits increased dramatically, as they generally do coming out of a recession.

Meanwhile, while waiting for the magic of supply side to happen, Republicans added more than $2 trillion to the national debt.

In sum, the Bush tax cuts delivered an extremely modest economic boost at a highly significant cost, to the tune of about $240 billion a year in missing revenue. The most economically destructive elements of the tax cuts—the marriage penalty relief and the child tax credits—are also the most politically popular, so they're likely to endure. At the same time, the elements that delivered a small economic tailwind—the dividend and capital-gains tax cuts, along with the lower marginal tax rate cuts—could be the first to be jettisoned under a Democratic regime (we hope not).

Can We Afford It?

Income inequality is another great way to ruin the cohesion of the nation. And wow, do we have income inequality! The richest 1 percent of Americans own 33 percent of all privately held wealth (assets minus liabilities) in our country. Putting aside their mansions, they own 40 percent of our nation's private liquid assets, including 44 percent of all stock and mutual funds, 58 percent of financial securities, 57 percent of business equity, and 35 percent of all nonresidential real estate, according to Professor Edward Wolff of New York University. They own more wealth than all of the bottom 90 percent of our country put together. They receive 20 percent of all annual income—a level not seen since the Great Depression. The average CEO earns 531 times the average factory worker—up from 42 times that level in 1960.

You might think from this litany that we have some animus against the wealthy. This is untrue. We don't begrudge them their money in the least—in fact, we earnestly aspire to be as rich as possible. Nevertheless, this degree of income inequality is not lovely to behold. It makes the rest of the United States look like a private game preserve for the superrich, who lead lives of extraordinary privilege in a parallel reality to the rest of us.

Here is the big secret of the truly rich: They're the only group that can afford to pay higher taxes without suffering adverse economic consequences. So naturally, the rich have had their taxes cut.

In a nation with stupendous deficits run up even at the peak of a business cycle (which we're now past), with forecast deficits of nuclear-disaster status, how can it be important to repeal the estate tax or to cut marginal tax rates on the wealthiest among us at this time? Isn't there enough income and wealth inequality in America already? Don't we need the revenue? Under the present circumstances, absent a recession, how does cutting taxes make social, moral, or fiscal policy sense? How does this bind the nation together in a time of war?

Punishing a Vital Industry

America's oil companies, besieged by foreign dictators, attacked endlessly in the media, and mocked and belittled in the academic world, are vital to the survival of this country. Just try to imagine America without oil—we'd be embroiled in *Mad Max*–style chaos within a week. We'd be living in complete anarchy.

Instead, we have a rich, advanced nation where the whole society and its progress float on liberally supplied, market-priced petroleum. And, like surly teenagers who hate their parents because they're totally dependent on them, we respond by hating the oil companies.

The oil companies aren't run by rich conspirators out of some crackpot Oliver Stone movie. They're not monopolists illegally fixing prices the way Rockefeller did more than a century ago. They're owned by people like us, employing people like us, and saving the rear ends of people like us.

If they're making a legal product that we can't live without in a legal way and selling it at a legal price, let's lay off them and let them do their jobs. If you think the oil companies make too much money for their stockholders, then buy their stock.

Instead, executives of the big oil companies are routinely hauled before Congressional committees whenever the price of gas goes up at the pump. No one has been able to prove price-fixing. The Federal Trade Commission specifically studied the subject, and found neither price-fixing nor gouging by any major oil company. The politicians know this. The hearings are just window dressing to make them look tough for their constituents. If they wanted to do something tough, they could open various U.S. lands for drilling or authorize nuclear power plants. That would take a small measure of courage in the face of the environmentalist onslaught. But why tackle a tough issue when you can get votes just by pretending?

The energy companies don't set the price of oil or of gasoline. What we pay for heating oil or gasoline isn't set in boardrooms in Texas but in trading rooms at commodities markets all over the world. Gas prices aren't set in shadowy conferences in shooting lodges, but in rooms of people shouting or punching computer keys in London, New York, and Tokyo. Oil is a world commodity like tin, copper, rubber, or coffee. The price is set by traders anticipating supply and demand. Rumors of war in the Middle East, terrorism against oil platforms in Nigeria, warmer weather in New England, bitter cold in London—these are what set energy prices. It's just like what happens on the stock markets every trading day: greed and fear at work. The oil companies can either lose or gain from this trading. Even the biggest U.S. energy companies are tiny pawns in the game compared with the world market.

If oil companies are trying to fix prices, they aren't very good at it. Only a few years ago, crude oil prices were below $10 a barrel, and prices today are considerably below their peak in the early 1980s, when adjusted for inflation. In addition, oil stocks are today 10 percent below their value before Katrina hit, and yet oil prices rose after the hurricane.

Posturing politicians love the idea of "windfall-profits taxes" on energy companies. These would presumably mandate a desirable level of corporate profits in one sector on which we depend. (And how long do you think it would apply to only this industry?) If profits exceeded that level, they'd be taxed. Of course, there's no plan to give a rebate to the companies if their profits have fallen below that desired level. A windfall-profits tax is an idea that has been tried and failed miserably. Why don't we raise an eyebrow when hedge funds make huge profits by moving around pieces of

paper and roiling markets—creating no social good—
but raise a ruckus when oil companies make profits
while keeping the whole nation going?

What is an oil company anyway? Consider Exxon
Mobil, the largest domestic oil company and the largest
stockholder-owned oil company in the world (although
far smaller than many state-owned oil companies such
as Aramco or Pemex).

Exxon Mobil has about 85,000 employees. An over-
whelming majority are working in oil fields producing
oil, working in refineries making gasoline and heating
oil from crude oil, shipping oil on large ships, taking
orders for energy products, filling out forms, and making sure machinery doesn't break down. It's demon-
strable that many retirement funds hold a great deal
of oil stocks, including Exxon Mobil. Of the other own-
ers, the largest holdings by far are at mutual funds and
exchange-traded funds—generally vehicles for middle-
class investors and retirees.

Columbia economics Professor C. Lowell Harriss
was fond of pointing out in his lectures: "Now, when
I say 'corporate shareholders,' think 'widows and
orphans.'" One of the largest holders is the College

Retirement Equities Fund, for higher-education teach-ers and others. Are we angry at them? If teachers get a bigger retirement because oil company profits are up, are we sad? So when gasoline and heating-oil prices increase, are we mad at the schoolteachers and retired police officers who own Exxon Mobil?

In other words, the plan is to send this message to energy-company investors, including retirees and pension funds: "Yes, we are in a situation of oil and gas shortage. Yes, we want you to risk billions of dollars exploring for, producing, and refining oil and process-ing gas. But if you succeed for any reason, and even if no price-fixing is found, we will punish you for it."

This is a sure way to commit national suicide.

Afterword

☆ ☆

In addition to all of the foregoing, let's talk about obscenity. There's something obscene about the truth that while soldiers are offering up their lives in Iraq and Afghanistan for what's basically minimum wage, hedge-fund operators and speculators are driving stakes through the hearts of Americans' retirement hopes and plans—and making billions at it. There's something obscene about having legions of homeless in the streets of our cities while a few blocks away men and women have $10 million weddings and children's birthday parties.

There's something obscene about the truth that the real power in America today is held by the finance potentates who add no value but only stoke fear and attempt to satisfy their bottomless greed. The major political might is owned by these people whether they're Democrats or Republicans, and there's no end in sight.

This is a great country, the greatest thing that has ever happened in man's bleak history. But we can destroy it by ruining our education system, wrecking our culture, devaluing the military, mocking religion . . . and by exalting pornography, especially the pornography of greed and power mixed together with a complete lack of empathy.

It is by no means too late. We can save ourselves. But to do it, we have to keep faith with the men and women who fight in Iraq and Afghanistan, who sleep at Arlington National Cemetery, and their families and their progeny.

We can do it if we know what we're fighting for: the last, best hope of mankind; the shimmering, shining city on a hill; this glorious land of the free and the brave; this bastion of hope and equality; this place where all the hopes of decent mankind reside. We can do it if we remember this one simple truth from John F. Kennedy: "Here on earth, God's work must truly be our own."

★   ★   ★

Acknowledgment

The authors are grateful beyond words to Adam M. Foster, research assistant at the American Enterprise Institute, for his many contributions to this book.

★　★　★

About the Authors

Ben Stein can be seen talking about finance on Fox TV news every week and writing about it regularly in *The New York Times* Sunday Business section. No wonder: Not only is he the son of the world-famous economist and government advisor Herbert Stein, but Ben is a respected economist in his own right. He received his B.A. with honors in economics from Columbia University in 1966, studied economics in the graduate school of economics at Yale while he earned his law degree there, and worked as an economist for the Department of Commerce.

Ben Stein is known to many as a movie and television personality, especially from *Ferris Bueller's Day Off* and from his long-running quiz show, *Win Ben Stein's Money.* But he has probably worked more in personal and corporate finance than anything else. He has written about finance for *Barron's* and *The Wall Street Journal* for decades. He was one of the chief busters of the junk-bond frauds of the 1980s, has been a longtime critic of corporate executives' self-dealing, and has co-written eight self-help books about personal finance. He frequently travels the country speaking about finance in both serious and humorous ways and is a regular contributor to the *CBS News Sunday Morning* and Fox News Network.

Website: **www.benstein.com**

Phil DeMuth was the valedictorian of his class at the University of California–Santa Barbara in 1972, then took his master's in communications and Ph.D. in clinical psychology. Both a psychologist and an investment adviser, Phil has written for *The Wall Street Journal, Barron's,* the *Louis Rukeyser Newsletter,* the *Journal of Financial Planning,* and **forbes.com**, as well as *Human Behavior* and *Psychology*

Today. His opinions have been quoted in **theStreet.com**, *Yahoo! Finance, On Wall Street,* and *Fortune* magazine, and he has been profiled in *Research* magazine and seen on *Forbes on Fox* and *Wall Street Week, CNBC's Squawk Box,* and *Kudlow & Company.* He is managing director of Conservative Wealth Management LLC in Los Angeles, a registered investment advisor to high-net-worth individuals, institutions, and foundations.

Website: **www.phildemuth.com**

Notes

☆ ☆

Notes

☆ ☆

Notes

☆ ☆

Notes

☆ ☆

NBP

We hope you enjoyed this book. If you'd
like additional information, please contact
New Beginnings Press through their distributors:

Hay House, Inc.
P.O. Box 5100
Carlsbad, CA 92018-5100

(760) 431-7695 or **(800) 654-5126**
(760) 431-6948 (fax) or **(800) 650-5115 (fax)**
www.hayhouse.com® • **www.hayfoundation.org**

✯   ✯   ✯

Distributed in Australia by: Hay House Australia Pty.
Ltd. 18/36 Ralph St. • Alexandria NSW 2015 • *Phone:*
612-9669-4299 • *Fax:* 612-9669-4144
www.hayhouse.com.au

Distributed in the United Kingdom by: Hay House UK, Ltd.
292B Kensal Rd., London W10 5BE • *Phone:*
44-20-8962-1230 • *Fax:* 44-20-8962-1239
www.hayhouse.co.uk

Distributed in the Republic of South Africa by:
Hay House SA (Pty), Ltd., P.O. Box 990, Witkoppen 2068
Phone/Fax: 27-11-467-8904 • orders@psdprom.co.za
www.hayhouse.co.za

Distributed in India by: Hay House Publishers India, Muskaan
Complex, Plot No. 3, B-2, Vasant Kunj, New Delhi 110 070 • *Phone:*
91-11-4176-1620 • *Fax:* 91-11-4176-1630 • www.hayhouse.co.in

Distributed in Canada by: Raincoast • 9050 Shaughnessy St.,
Vancouver, B.C. V6P 6E5 • *Phone:* (604) 323-7100
Fax: (604) 323-2600

✷   ✷   ✷